Growing Up in Christ

growing up in CHRIST

A Guide for Families with Adolescents

by

Eugene H. Peterson

Speaking the truth in love, we are to grow up in every way into him
who is the head, into Christ. Ephesians 4:15

JOHN KNOX PRESS
ATLANTA

Parts of chapters 2, 4, 5, 8, and 9 have been previously published by Success With Youth Publications, Inc., 421 West Southern Avenue, Tempe, Arizona 85282. They are used with permission.

Library of Congress Cataloging in Publication Data

Peterson, Eugene H   1932–
  Growing up in Christ.

  Includes bibliographical references.
  1. Youth—Religious life. 2. Parent and child.
I. Title.
BV4531.2.P485   248′.83   76–12396
ISBN 0–8042–2026–3

For my mother and father
who made a home where
growing up and growing up
in Christ
were always the same thing

We make the simplest and yet at the same time the most comprehensive statement when we say that it is the parents' responsibility to give their children the opportunity to encounter the God who is present, operative and revealed in Jesus Christ, to know Him and to learn to love and fear Him. The greatest and smallest things, the most serious and the most trivial, which can happen between parents and children, can become for parents an occasion to present to their children this opportunity. No one else has so many manifold and intimate occasions over what is normally so long and continuous a stretch of time to put this opportunity before another human being as do parents in relation to their children. And no one again has these occasions at a period which is so formative and usually so decisive and fundamental. This time and its opportunities must not be missed.

Karl Barth[1]

Contents

Introduction

Growing up—becoming mature—is a Christian process. It is also, of course, biological, social, and emotional. But mostly it is Christian: the development of mature relationships between God and persons in a community of faith. "Growing up in Christ" centers and models all growing up.

Adolescents exhibit the coming of age process in a particularly vivid form. And their parents are unavoidably involved in it. These parents of adolescents are in a particularly advantageous position to use the growing-up process in personal ways, putting it to use for the glory of God. But parents don't always look at it that way. As their pastor, I have gathered some of these parents together from time to time in order to use our common experience with the adolescent in our own growth in Christ.

My purpose is to develop a sense of Christian discipleship among parents of youth in the areas where the parents' needs are thickest and their sense of competence, perhaps, thinnest. The persons ordinarily most concerned with youth are their fathers and mothers. They have the most invested. Many others share the interest and concern—excellent youth ministries have been developed in the church and many specialist groups carry out effective ministries to and among the adolescent. Specialists, though, come and go: the parents are a constant, year after year, generation after generation. It is an important and recurrent ministry of the church to develop hope and trust among these parents of youth, nurturing concepts of Christian growth and encouraging the gifts of guidance. It is also important to direct whatever is acquired back into the family, and not divert it somewhere else. For the family is a most useful, maybe *the* most useful, arena in which to learn the faith: "Family life is like a hall endowed with the finest acoustical properties. Growing children hear not only their parents' words (and in most cases gradually ignore them), they hear the intentions, the attitudes behind the words. Above all they learn what their parents *really* admire, *really* despise."[1]

The Parent Coalition

Prior to adolescence, parents are used to being in nearly total control of their children. They are both stronger and wiser during those years. Parental strength and wisdom are necessary to the child's survival. The child needs, rarely questions, and ordinarily appreciates the physical protection, the intelligent guidance, and the emotional warmth of parents. Adolescence, though, abruptly introduces new factors. Needs are now present for which the old strengths are not adequate. The stable supply-demand equilibrium which worked throughout childhood is thrown into disorder—the market goes haywire. And parents do not improve family life by doing more vehemently the same things they have done all along. Strength and wisdom which were adequate through childhood years no longer work. New ways of sharing strength and new ways of communicating insight are needed. In order that we may function adequately as parents to an adolescent, new skills have to be developed. These skills cannot be packaged by the church and purchased by the parent; they can, though, be developed in a community of persons who share a common task and rely on a common faith. A small group is an excellent format for accomplishing this: it provides a structure for giving attention to the task at hand and develops a community of ministry among parents.

The behind-the-scenes premise for doing this is described in the church's doctrine of the "priesthood of all believers" by which each Christian discovers ways in which she or he functions as a priest to another and lets the other act in priestly ways in return. If someone steps in and assumes the role of an expert who is going to instruct parents in the mysteries of adolescence, there can be no community, only a classroom. If the parents assume the role of victims who are going to get rescued by an expert, there can be no community, only a first-aid station. But if parents, pastors, and others who have responsibilities with youth, join in sharing their troubles and insights, their concerns and strengths, they can become a community, "fellow heirs, members of the same body, and partakers of the promise in Christ Jesus through the gospel." (Ephesians 3:6) The normal way for Christians to grow in strength and competence is in just such community. God does not, it appears from the Biblical record, intend that the Christian deal with life alone—we are "members of one another." When parents are in community with others who share similar responsibilities and who believe in a similar grace, there is growth. They discover that they are not the first or the only ones who are doing a less-than-perfect job dealing with the adolescent in their home. They realize, as C. S. Lewis once wrote to a troubled parent, that the "only 'ordinary' homes seem to be the ones we don't know much about, just as the only blue mountains are those 10 miles away."[2] A parent group gives visibility to both the strength and weakness in other homes and puts the members in touch with one another during the years when they experience the stress that is a by-product of their children's adolescence.

Parents, pastors, and other adults who have responsibilities with youth are natural allies in this ministry, and quickly learn to function as priests to each other when provided with the opportunity. They all bear major responsibilities. When they share needs and strengths, they form a coalition which makes for a far stronger ministry than if any tried to go it alone. Parents don't ordinarily think of themselves as participants in ministry or as having anything to offer to others. They think of themselves in defeatist terms: they are frustrated and bewildered, and look to the professional for help in doing for their sons and daughters what they feel they cannot do. If leaders simply respond to parental requests, they will alleviate some symptoms, but they will barely touch the need. The need is to share a ministry with parents, a ministry that is able to nurture the new life which is forming in the adolescent personality.

The Gift of Adolescence

Parents who engage to form a "priesthood coalition" find it easy to converse about their common needs. Their shared investment in the adolescent process provides experiences which rapidly put them in touch with each other. But they also have common gifts: the children they are rearing are, each of them, gifts of God. It is important to articulate this area of commonality, for while it is certainly true that the adolescent is a gift, it is not at all obvious.

When I hear the sentence "children are a gift of God," images of cuddly, gurgling infants, and well-scrubbed boys and girls in happy play rush into my mind. It never occurs to me to think of sullen adolescents—door-slamming fifteen-year-old daughters, or defiantly argumentative sixteen-year-old sons.

Infants are manifestly God's gifts. In them God brings into our lives a sense of miracle, a mood of wonder, a conviction of worth, a readiness to grasp responsibility. At the very time in life (young adulthood) when it is most easy to suppose that *we* are in control, that the world owes us a living, that through our education and training we have reduced our environment to something manageable—at this time God gives us a child to restore our sense of creaturehood, our own sense of being a child of God. Only very stubborn unbelievers can be in the presence of a newborn infant and maintain the arrogant pose that they are the creator, the ruler, and the maker. For these few moments, at least, when the child is freshly upon us, it is hardly possible to reduce our experience to the explanations of biology or the diagrams of sex education. The simple fact of life is far beyond anything we can engineer, control, or explain. And we ourselves become aware of our creaturehood—not makers, not managers, not mothers, not fathers, but *children* of God. We apprehend the world through the forms of infancy and we are in Eden again. We discover elemental reality: we find what it means to care, to nurture, to respond. The delights of touch, sound, sight fill the day. We see what God has created, how he loves, the designs of his providence, his glory. The infant is a gift of God by which we are given stimulus and example in the forms of childlikeness which are prerequisite to entering the kingdom of God.

But the adolescent, though it may not be obvious, is no less a gift of God. The infant is God's gift to the young adult; the adolescent is a similar gift to the middle-aged, for the adolescent is "born" into our lives during our middle decades (when we are in our thirties, forties, and fifties). These middle decades of life are the very times when we are prone to stagnation and depression, when the wonders of life are all banalities and the juices of life are drying up. For many there is a feeling of letdown. The surging strength of early adulthood has not carried us to eminence. There have been enough failures and disappointments to accumulate in a thoroughgoing fatigue. Even when there is outward success, there is often a corresponding inner dryness, a sensation of hollowness, a shriveling of the hopes, the ideals, and the expectations of earlier years.

> What I had not foreseen
> Was the gradual day
> Weakening the will
> Leaking the brightness away.
>
> Stephen Spender[3]

And then God's gift: in the rather awkward packaging of the adolescent God brings into our lives a challenge to grow, a testing of love, a deepening of hope, a realization of newness. It comes at just the right time. All the realities that have become hackneyed and trite suddenly are in fresh form before us, demanding response, requiring participation.

The French talk of a *deformation professionelle*—a liability, a tendency to defect, that is inherent in the role one has assumed as, say, a physician, a lawyer, a priest. If there is a *deformation* to which the middle-aged are subject, it is the assumption that, because they have completed their growth biologically and have certification of their growth educationally and professionally, there is no more growing to be done. They develop a blind spot concerning personal growth. Growth is that which has to be gotten through in order to get to be an adult: "Oh, hurry and grow up, won't you!" Growth is the delight of the young and the agony of youth, but it is not personal to the middle-aged. That is the blind spot fatal to Christian discipleship. An adolescent, by challenging and testing personal relationships in numerous ways, opens our eyes to growth in ourselves. The very nature of relationship with God has growth at its center. Scripture, describing our life with God, uses metaphors of "growth" continually and repeatedly. There is no point at which we become exempt from the realities of "growing up in Christ."

Adolescents are, more than anything else, growing up—and they will not do it quietly. They will not stay in their room and do their growing in isolation; they will not restrict their growing to the times when they are safely among peers. Their growing spills out, unsystematically, all over the place. But in this way adolescents, energetically modeling and insistently stimulating growth, are God's gift to parents who are in danger of being arrested in their own growth.

Parents can, of course, even in the face of this, refuse to grow. They can say, "I have completed my growing up; I know what it means to be a person, a Christian, a citizen, a man, a woman. And I am going to preside over your growing up. I will provide the guidelines, I will make the rules, I will determine the course of your growth." Such a position can be either benevolent or despotic, but it is, in either case, detached. The parents have removed themselves from the processes of growth and only observe and preside over the growth of the child. Or the parents can disqualify themselves from further growth by saying, "I've made such a mess of my own growing up that I am not going to share in yours—I gave up on my own life years ago. I'll do the best I can for you, I'll help where I can, but don't expect me to grow: I'm not much good as a Christian, or even as a person. I just don't have the energy to go through the agony of growing up any more." The stance may appear to be full of humility and modesty; in effect, it is a capitulation to despair. It is a begging off of another chance at becoming a mature person in Christ.

Parents of adolescents, it seems to me, are not best characterized as people who do the right things or say the right things, but as ones who plunge into the process of growth. It will be a different style of growth from what goes on in adolescence, but it will be growth nevertheless. John Henry Newman wrote: "In a higher world it is otherwise, but here below to live is to change, and to be perfect is to have changed often."[4] He was writing about the growth of doctrine, but his words are quite as appropriate for growth in parents. If the parent will accept the adolescent as a gift from God, there will be bright new areas of hope which will open up, fresh energies of love released, vital surges of faith.

When I mentally review the families where parents seem to be doing a good job of living the Christian faith in relation to their children, it is quickly apparent that actual practices vary widely. Particular rules, techniques of discipline, variations in strictness and permissiveness—they run the gamut. One thing stands out:

these parents seriously, honestly, joyfully follow the way of Christ themselves. They don't focus on youth as "a problem" and try to solve it. They are engaged in vigorous Christian growth on their own and permit their children to look over their shoulders while they do it. It is the old practice of apprenticeship applied to family life. The young apprentice is placed in close association with a master craftsman for a period of years. Through the association he shares a discipline, learns skills, and discusses the work. He sees the master at his best and his worst. He sees him make mistakes and sees how he reacts to his mistakes. The master craftsman may not be a good educational psychologist and he certainly need not be a perfect man, but he has to be good at what he is doing. Likewise the parents. They don't have to be experts in psychology or have read the latest book on adolescent emotions. And they don't have to live perfect lives, but they must take seriously what they are doing—which is growing up in Christ. They must do it openly before youth so that the youth can observe, imitate, and make their mistakes in the context of care.

The task of the parent, in other words, is not directly to confront the problems of the young and find the best solutions to them. It is to confront life, and Christ in life, and deal with that. A parent's main job is not to be a parent but to be a person. There are no techniques to master which will make a good parent. There is no book to read which will give the right answers. The parent's main task is to give a living demonstration that adulthood is full, alive, and Christian.

Procedures and Format for a Parent Group

Having concluded that adolescence is not a problem to be solved, or a mystery to be unraveled, or a difficulty to be mastered, but simply a gift to be accepted, I have thought that I could encourage parents to accept it by doing two things: gathering a community of Christians similarly situated in which the gift could be appreciated, and providing guidance in dealing with the areas of growth which adolescents characteristically open up for us.

As to procedures: I invite, either by letter or personal visit, the parents of adolescents in my parish to become members of a small group that will meet for ten sessions. I announce that the purpose of the group will be to gather and focus the resources of our Christian community in relation to their parental task, a task I assume has some added demands upon it at this time in their lives.

I make it clear that this is not a series of lectures in which I will instruct them in how to be better parents, but that it is a group, a gathering of the people of God, in which we will share our strengths and weaknesses, our insights and needs, among brothers and sisters in the faith who are involved in common parent experiences with adolescence.

When the group assembles for the first time, I let them establish the frequency, the time, and the place of subsequent meetings. And I go over the following ground rules.

    1. Start and stop at an agreed-upon time. Even if the discussion is going great, stop when you said you would. There will be another session. Late-night bull-sessions are for people who don't have to go to work on the next day.

    2. Don't dominate. Some people, if they don't watch themselves, take over a group. If you are one of those kind, discipline yourself. Instead of always giving your own opinions, try asking a few questions of quieter members of the group, drawing them into more participation.

    3. Take the group seriously. Give it high priority. Refuse to let anything but illness keep you from it. Sporadic attendance weakens the group. Since each person is part of the content, the group won't function well without you.

    4. Don't gossip. What goes on in the group should stay in the group. This isn't material to be discussed with the neighbors over coffee. The group is an extension of the people of God in the church in which friends are sharing important aspects of their life in Christ in a spirit of confidence and prayer.

    5. Take the Lord seriously. He is more interested in you and your children than you are. Open yourself to the strength he provides in Jesus Christ. Find some time during each session, either as you begin or as you conclude, to express this openness to God in prayer.

The material for guidance has this format: First there is a statement of the *theme*. I begin the session with that, announcing it and sometimes elaborating briefly. The *questions* which follow develop group discussion and interchange. The parents will provide the most important content. Growth will come out of these exchanges as they function in ministry to one another. The *comment* which concludes each section is a fusion of conversations and ideas which have come out of groups I have led. It is not a lecture to be delivered. It is, rather, what I find useful to have available in my mind as I am leader-participant in the group. Sometimes I say very little of it. Other times more. At no time all of it. It is a gathering of conversations and insights from many parents out of many groups; I stock my mind with it so that the material is readily accessible for guidance and perspective in the group.

It is possible, of course, to use this material more privately within the "nuclear" family, developing growth in an interchange between adult parents and adolescent children. In actual fact many of these insights and conversations originated in my own home, without benefit of other parents, and so if you simply alter the form of the questions, the insights should be readily adaptable for use within the individual family again. But still I think it preferable, more in keeping with the Biblical mode, and worth whatever effort it requires, to expand the discussion so that it includes other parents who are brothers and sisters in Christ.

"I'll Dress
I   the Way I Want!"

Adolescence is the time when we *become* ourselves. The experiences and training of childhood are reformulated and individualized into a personal identity. Parents have much less control over the process than they would like, and their loss of control causes anxiety. But adolescence is not an affliction: it is a healthy process of growth, which the Christian can approach with good hope.

* * * * * * * *

1. Tell the group about yourself: what kind of jobs you have had, where you grew up, things that stand out in the last thirty years of your personal history.
2. What kind of adolescence did you have? As you look back on it what still interests you? Do you remember how others in your family, brothers and sisters, went through their adolescence?
3. Describe your teenager to the group. What are his or her characteristics? What changes have you noticed as she or he has entered adolescence? What good things have appeared? What difficulties have come up? In what ways are you disappointed?
4. Read 1 Samuel 3. Do you see a way in which this can be read as a description of adolescent growth?
5. Erik Erikson, an exceptionally wise observer of the adolescent process, wrote: ". . . there is a 'natural' period of uprootedness in human life: adolescence. Like a trapeze artist, the young person in the middle of vigorous motion must let go of his safe hold on childhood and reach out for a firm grasp on adulthood, depending for a breathless interval on a relatedness between the past and the future, and on the reliability of those he must let go of, and those who will 'receive' him."[1] Can you offer some illustration of that statement from the life of your teenager?
6. How have you changed in the last few years? Do you see yourself differently now from the way you did, say, ten

or five years ago? How does your self-concept in middle
age compare and differ from what you remember from
adolescence?

✳ ✳ ✳ ✳ ✳ ✳ ✳ ✳

Adolescents are involved, nearly full-time, in discovering who
they are. Maybe that is why they spend so much time in front of
the mirror. The process of self-definition goes on day and night. It
is a process full of awkward agonies:

> . . . the distress
> Of boyhood changing into man;
> The unfinished man and his pain
> Brought face to face with his own clumsiness.
> W. B. Yeats[2]

Through the years of childhood parents severely circumscribe
the exercise of free will. Children are free to arrange blocks the way
they wish; they are not free to arrange the furniture. They are
allowed to choose whether to wear blue or red shirts to school; they
are not allowed to choose whether to go to school or not. The
essential, life-significant matters are out of reach of their will. When
a decision would affect their own future or the community's comfort they are not permitted to make a choice.

But at adolescence the children begin to demand more and more
of a voice in decisions. Their bodies develop sexual maturity, their
minds develop intellective agility, their emotions develop sensitivity and variety. They are within sight of adult life, the time when
they will *have* to make their choices independently and live responsibly with them, and they want to get started. The task of adolescence is to learn how to make decisions and to become accustomed
to the identity the decisions produce. As such they cannot be the
parents' decisions. They have to be different from, apart from,
sometimes in contrast to, the decisions of the parents. As the young
person develops capacity to make responsible decisions these decisions provide the raw material for self-identity. The adolescent who
says, "I am free to choose this way of life" is then able to say, "I am
the person who has made these choices." Identity is the product of
decisions. Each adolescent makes the decisions that produce the life

that is uniquely his, or hers. Each of them becomes the person who
made those decisions. As they gain strength in choosing, each of
them accumulates an assurance of being herself, or himself, and no
other.

In early adolescence there is a great deal of fuzziness in self-
identity. Youth hides this either by projecting an identity derived
from a hero, or assimilating into a group. The nationwide sameness
in the dress and language of the young is protective armor. But as
adolescents mature and gain skill in making decisions they will
gradually be able to recognize their own individuality. Each of them
will be able to say, "This is me." Younger adolescents all seem to
look and sound alike. As they move to later years they become more
able to let themselves be seen as differentiated persons. Insofar as
they are not able to do that they fail to complete the adolescent task.

It is not a smooth process. It staggers and lurches. It mysteriously
alternates brisk strides with sulking slouches. There are tentative,
obviously immature, ventures. Youth often practice defining themselves by demonstrating what they are not: they are not, for instance, what their parents say they are. They provide evidence in
hair and clothing styles which differ from what parents choose.
Sometimes self-assertion is vehement. When parents resist there is
defiance: "I'll dress the way I want!" But if parents let this kind of
conflict dominate the relationship, youth will conclude that the
parents are not concerned with the deeper developments stirring
beneath the surface, but only in what others are going to say or
think. In such cases youth have a real grievance: they ought to be
able to expect more from parents.

In 1 Samuel 3 this aspect of adolescent development is told in a
way that gives parents usable insights into what their son or daughter is going through, and encourages deep respect toward it. It is
particularly useful because it places the adolescent experience in a
theological setting—both the human experience and the spiritual
reality are accounted for. That is what makes the story, brief as it
is, so valuable. For the parent has no end of psychologists, sociolo-
gists, ethnologists, and anthropologists who are willing to tell what
"coming of age" means. Their writings are full of good information
and often sparkle with insight. But they do not give space to that
which is primary for the Christian parent—the promises of God

and the call of God. Good theologians must have a thorough knowledge of human nature and be continuously in touch with it as they
narrate the nature and activity of God. The theologian who wrote
1 Samuel 3 was especially good: the incident of the young man
Samuel in the temple establishes the significant adolescent experience of identify-formation in the context of the revelation of God.
Samuel had been placed in the temple at an early age by his
grateful parents, Elkanah and Hannah. He spent his childhood
years growing up in association with the priest Eli, who seems to
have acted as a kind of foster parent. We get the feeling that Samuel
was thoroughly at home in the temple, and that he was accustomed
to running errands and taking care of Eli's needs. Samuel can be
seen as a fairly typical child, dedicated to God by his parents, provided with a religious environment to grow up in, and feeling quite
comfortable with the arrangement.

When Samuel first heard the voice calling his name in the night
he assumed it was the voice he had been used to hearing through
his childhood years—the voice of command, the voice of guidance,
the voice of instruction. He responded as he always had. But the
response did not work. There was no connection between the voice
and his customary response. His answer produced no communication, no meaning.

Then Eli, who knew something of what happens in adolescence,
and who functions in the story in a dual role as parent and priest,
instructed him to respond to the voice not as to the call of a father
but as to the call of God. Eli sensed that Samuel had reached the
point in his life when he was ready to respond in his own right to
God. No longer was his life to be controlled by temple routines and
parental guidance. No longer was his life a derivation of the dedica-
tion of his parents and the guidance of "religion." There was now
a voice of the living God, personal and direct. It was not a voice that
either parent or priest could mediate for him. He heard it himself.

The center of the story is the emphatic pronunciation of the
personal name, "Samuel! Samuel!" That naming tells us nearly all
we need to know about adolescence. It tells us that the meaning, the
identity, of the person is raised to a new level—emphasized and
defined. The name is the most personal form of address. It is that
which evokes a response in us. Our name is the most personal word

which can be said to or about us. Eugen Rosenstock-Huessy, who has provided brilliant insights into the grammar of "naming," writes: "The name is the state of speech in which we do not speak of people or things or values, but in which we speak *to* people, things, and values. . . . The name is the right address of a person under which he or she will respond. The original meaning of language was this very fact that it could be used to make people respond."[3]

Adolescence is never categorical—it is not a pigeonhole we can place people in when we don't quite understand what they are doing; it can never be reduced to "a phase you are going through." Generalities can be averred but what matters is always detailed and personal. It is the evocation of a name. Much of the behavior of youth is an attempt to get across to adult society not that they are different, but that they want to be. They want to be recognized, each of them wants to be noticed, as person, not as representative of a class, not as an instance of adolescence, but as someone with a name. The name brings recognition that I am this person and not another. My being cannot be explained by parents or priests or teachers. It is *sui generis.*

This naming is at the center of adolescence, but the *hearing* of the name is only half of the meaning; the other half is that Samuel acknowledged that *God* was calling his name. His childhood blossomed into adulthood under the auspices of God's call. It is when he recognizes himself as one named by God that he finds the full content of "Samuel." Not a child of Elkanah and Hannah, not the ward of Eli, but the one God calls by personal name.

This provides a window through which the Christian can see that the most significant reality in adolescent development is a relationship with God. It is not their sexuality, not their mind, not their social relationships, not their emotions that are at the center—it is God. The adolescent becomes aware of the Beyond, of being in a cosmos, of being a child of eternity, of facing ultimates, of being in a world of spiritual reality and moral significance. The adolescent becomes conscious of these realities in conjunction with discovering his or her personal identity. As adolescents learn to make choices that affirm their own identity, responding to the content of their names, they are doing it in response to the God who has identified them, the God who pronounces those names.

The adolescent is, in fact, acquiring firsthand experience in the church's doctrine of election. Theologians differ in how they understand this doctrine, but all agree that it arises out of recognition that God *chooses,* that there is a free, decision-making activity in God and that it is exercised in relation to persons. Election means that God freely decides things and that the decisions make a significant (eternal) difference.

As Samuel responded to the voice of God he found himself plunged into a world which was *elective.* And so do all youth. We live in a world where God is active in choosing us and where our highest acts are a response to that choice, saying "yes" to God's "yes." In this environment decision making can never be trivial or peripheral. Every choice that youth make—even choices on seemingly insubstantial affairs like hairstyle and clothing—is part of a process in which they are learning to make the choices which will make them what they will be in Christ.

Adolescent decisions are made in the context of the divine election. They are not, as some suppose, muddled spasms of self-will which evolve into "fulfilling your potential." And they must not be a monitored parody of choices which become "following your father's footsteps." No real identity is formed in such decisions. What Christian gospel is there in telling an adolescent to become what he or she potentially is when much of that potential is destructive and not a little of it sordid? And what good news is there in insisting on an identity formed on the model of the parent, however good that model? No youth who want to become adults want to "have it made" for them. They want to make it—they want their own decisions to have significance.

In such a way the young Samuel is a paradigm for the adolescent experience: he hears his name pronounced in a new way, a way that calls forth his identity; eventually he recognizes that it is God who is pronouncing the name, that his new life is created in newness by God.

There is a definite implication in this for the parent: the parent is not in charge of the so-called identity crisis. The Samuel incident takes place at night, in solitude, away from both parents and peers. And Eli seems quite willing to trust Samuel to that solitude, to let him be private, away from his jurisdiction, separate from his super-vision while this awesome experience takes place. Every adolescent is entitled to this privacy. Adults, even when the adults are parents, have no right to pry. The process of self-definition is delicate and intricate; interference is rude and can be abortive. The acceptance of this implication will prevent the parent from joining those who take a "religious" position toward youth. The interest of these peo-ple is no doubt sincere, but it lacks the self-confidence and theologi-cal maturity to be a gospel. And it does nothing but damage. These people are usually in one of two groups.

One group sees youth as the great pagan force in the modern world: "Never, since the age of Constantine, has there been within Christendom such a self-conscious, self-perpetuating culture that does not accept or live by the assumptions of the Christian gospel. This alien society—some call it a 'counter culture'—is obviously in need of salvation. It is found in its purest form among youth. It is ignorant of Christianity as it is of most history. This mass of youth has been cut off from Biblical and Christian traditions by the rapid changes in culture and an immersion in technology and machines. They constitute a foreign land superimposed on the familiar geogra-phy of Christian civilization. They speak a language that is barely intelligible; they wear costumes that reflect little dignity. Their personal habits show no regard for the social amenities of cleanli-ness and health. They carry in their imagination no memory of human sin or virtue. They are like children in history, insisting on learning everything by trial and error—a kind of anti-historical, neolithic mentality. Experience is their authority. They are primi-tives with no past and no future, only a present. They are cut off from the hard-won lessons of moral truth and redemptive history rooted in the Biblical past and the Christian future." It is easy to look at this "neo-paganism" and talk of launching a special cam-paign to bring about conversion.

The other group looks at youth with wide-eyed naiveté and says: "No generation of Christians has so completely failed to live out the gospel as the present adult population. It has sleepily let itself be-come compromised by a depersonalized modernity which puts prime value on secular achievement and material progress. It has succumbed to a way of thinking which accepts military violence as a way of life and which has permitted the life of the spirit to be squeezed into tiny little corners while being dominated by nationalistic pride and personal greed. Covetousness (under camouflage of respectable terms like 'ambition' 'progress' and 'growth') is admired and encouraged while the earth is decimated and spirits atrophy. But the youth have suddenly emerged as a hope of salvation. Their search for personal integrity and meaning and their priorities for finding personal relationships under the banners of peace and love are a sign that they are in the vanguard of a personal (as against a technological) world where human values will again reign supreme. Their communes are an admirable search for authentic family life which the older generation let degenerate in front of the television set. Their drugs are a legitimate search for an exciting inner life which the older generation traded in on a new model car. Their clothes are an assertion of personal identity which the older generation relinquished to the uniform of the bureaucracy. Their music is a sign of commitment and involvement which the older generation apathetically dropped while being soothed with background mood music. Their sex is an attempt at openness and intensity in relationships which the older generation suppressed in straitjackets of convention and taboo. These youth are the hope of the future: their ideals are humane, and their insights are righteous. If they are deficient in morals and theology that is understandable—morals and theology didn't prevent us from getting into a series of wars and polluting the earth. Look to the youth as the fresh, unspoiled Galahads in quest of new life. Follow them. They will give us the 'greening of America.' "

The first group confidently condemns and is ready to march in with an answer. The second group guiltily confesses failure and waits, hopefully, for help. Christian parents do better to take a role that is both more modest and more effective: instead of meddling with the adolescents, either in zeal or in hope, they will, with Eli, refer them to God.

For one of the difficulties of parents is that they are, must be, outsiders to this process. They cannot do very much—at least not directly. Youth in process of "finding out who I am" use parents as a foil. Self-identity must be formed apart from the parent. Which means that the parent is going to feel left out, rejected, defied, and unappreciated. Parents cannot, as they are accustomed to doing through the childhood years, share each hurt and be closely involved in each detail. There *must* be some alienation during the adolescent years.

But if the parents are outsiders to the process of adolescence they do not have to be opponents of it. If they cannot be insiders sharing all the intricacies of growth they do not have to be belligerent or resentful. They can still be parents who are prayerful and interested, observing with intelligent sympathy and praying with knowledgeable confidence. And they can thank God for the adolescent stimulus to self-discovery and personal growth, which goads them from sluggish backwaters into the whitewater of the river of God where established maturities get infused with the vibrance and zest of discipleship.

"I'm Not Going 2 to Church!"

Adolescents, in an attempt to find the sources of their own being and arrive at self-definition, sometimes use the device of denial or rejection. In search of *personal* faith they reject everything that is *impersonal* or *institutional*. From their point of view that often means rejecting the church.

* * * * * * *

1. Did you resist going to church when you were an adolescent? How did your parents respond? How do you now evaluate what they did?

2. Did you ever drop out of the church completely? For how long did the drop-out period last? What factors brought about your return?

3. How do your teenagers express their resistance to the church? What reasons do they give? What tactics do they employ?

4. What do you say when they say or act out, "I'm not going to church"? Do you have a consistent strategy? What are your ground rules?

5. Why do you go to church? What does it mean to you? What does the actual act of worship mean to you personally? How is it important in your total life?

6. Why do you want your child to go to church, even when she or he doesn't feel like it?

* * * * * * *

Adolescent growth not uncommonly includes the threat of refusing to go to church: "I'm not going to church today!" When that threat is sounded it can trigger an avalanche of emotions in the Christian parent. Parents of an adolescent are involved, whether they like it or not, in the confusions of the adolescent. One of the difficult questions parents must deal with is: "How do I as a Christian parent fulfill my responsibility to help my teenager be a Christian—and does making him go to church help or hinder?" Parents have a lot at stake in the response their child makes to God. They have invested prayer, concern, training and love: they don't want to see it wiped out.

The task was clearer when the child was younger. Young children must be taught "line upon line and precept upon precept." They must be provided with faithful church associations. They must know what is in the Bible, that God loves them, and that they live in a moral universe where things count eternally. That is not always easy to do, but the task is fairly straightforward: the parent is a teacher and example of the faith; the child is learner and imitator.

But when the children become adolescents they are no longer primarily "learners" (although they are still learning); they now become more and more "deciders." They begin to practice making the decisions that will make it possible to live responsibly in an adult world in a few years. As the children shift their basic stance there must be a corresponding shift in parental response. The shifts put both in unfamiliar positions, feeling awkward and unsure.

What happens, for instance, when adolescent decisions deviate from those that the parent has made in regard to the church? Most parents are willing to allow for some diversity of decisions in regard to hairstyle, or clothes, or friends; but what do they do if things of fundamental and eternal importance are threatened with rejection? The parent is in a dilemma. Parents want the youth to learn to make adult decisions and get practice doing it with as little interference as possible. But are they being responsible in allowing this freedom to extend to an area as critical as the church?

Some parents think not. They believe that as long as the children share the parents' home they are bound to the parents' religion: "As long as you live under my roof you will go to church with the rest of the family. We'll not discuss it any more."

Other parents take essentially the same position but use pressure tactics to enforce it: "If you don't go to church today, you're not going bowling tomorrow night," or, "If you maintain a perfect attendance at church for the rest of the year I'll buy you a stereo for your room." Variations on the themes of bullying and bribery are endless.

Some parents give up the struggle. They give in to the persistent complaining and heel-dragging that makes every Sunday morning a scrimmage. They go to church minus a teenager but also without a headache. But in conceding the contest they often pick up feelings of guilt or failure. They have difficulty enjoying their peaceful drive to church.

Still other parents think that when adolescents begin questioning the faith of their fathers (or father!) it is a signal for the parent to begin to develop and make more explicit a new relationship—a relationship not of father and daughter, mother and son, but of two Christians. In addition to the responsibility of being a Christian *parent* there is a call now to be a Christian *person*, sharing the meaning of a personal faith.

Any child of moderate perception, having lived for over a decade under the same roof with parents, knows that just because they are Christians and go to church on Sundays does not mean they are also saints. The child knows they sin daily. Now is the time to talk about that. It is time for the parent, instead of just advising and commanding, occasionally, at least, to share personal Christian growth. Experiences of failure and discoveries of forgiveness can be shared. The child is in a position to understand a sense of pilgrimage, of not yet having arrived, of gratitude for grace. If parents insist on keeping up a front of religious imperturbability, unflappable faith, and absolute assurance, all they will do is widen the credibility gap.

It is a serious mistake to think that when questions arise and doubts and rebellions are expressed, the correct strategy is an intensified publicity campaign: "Families that pray together stay together . . . if you leave the church you are leaving the richest heritage of mankind . . . how do you expect God to bless you if you turn your back on him like this?" etc. No parent is required to mount an advertising campaign on behalf of the Deity.

One father, when confronted by a son who began expressing distaste for everything connected with the church and objecting to further participation, said something like this: "I remember having those feelings myself; in fact, I still have them from time to time. The only trouble, though, with staying away from church at a time like this is that there is no way to continue the conversation with others involved on the other side of some ideas and practices that obviously matter a great deal. For the first time in your life you're beginning to think and feel as an adult. Many of the things that you are finding distasteful are what you experienced as a child in the church. Wouldn't it be more reasonable to take your thinking and feeling into the sanctuary each Sunday for the next few years and test it out there? If you stay home you don't have anybody to argue with or test yourself against—except your childhood memories. You are changing and learning very rapidly now; the church needs your new vision and experience. You are having an argument with the church; in very few arguments is one person right and the other wrong. What one hopes for in an argument is that both persons will discover more deeply what the other is saying, appreciate it, and either be changed or modified by it. But this takes considerable listening, correcting bad impressions, re-assessing misjudged positions. Nobody would want you to swallow uncritically everything that is going on in the church, but if you walk out of the room the possibilities for adult, responsible debate are eliminated.

"The Christian church has always put a great deal of emphasis on your free decision in relation to God. Now that you are forming skills in making responsible, free decisions of your own it is important to me that you stay in the room while the conversation is going on so that your final decisions will be mature. I will respect any decisions that you eventually make, but right now I feel that any decision you made would be formed mostly out of childhood experience, and therefore would have little chance of expressing maturity.

"Let me give you an example. If you told me today that you hated girls and never wanted to associate with them again [the boy had just had a painful breakup with a girl friend] I think I would respect your feelings and understand something of what went into producing them. But on the basis of that feeling I wouldn't permit you to enter a celibate order in which you would never be able to have any contact with women again. There are still hang-ups to get over. There are tensions still unresolved. You deserve to have more adult experience behind you before you make that kind of decision. It would be better if you kept learning about girls and had some responsible relationships with them as you grow so that you develop some depth experience in the nature of the man-woman interaction.

"That is kind of the way it is with you and the church. Part of my responsibility as a parent is to try to keep you in the flow of experience as long as possible so that you feel as much and face as much as is there and so be equipped to make good, adult decisions. I would like you to share in the congregational life of worship and learning just as I do. I don't think you need to believe all of it, or be uncritical of any of it. There are many things in the church that are sinful and disobedient—if you can see what they are you will be of help to others. You may feel that the church doesn't appreciate your perspectives or your ideas; and in all honesty I must tell you that it might not. But *I* do and I would like to keep on hearing about them.

"Right now you have a fresh vision of the whole operation that adults long involved in its structure lack. It is important to have the benefit of your fresh insight. Part of the reason that you have this insight is that you don't have the long-range responsibilities and vested interests in things as they are. Those who have these responsibilities and interests, including me, don't find it easy to express some feelings or consider some ideas. Consequently your objectivity is valuable. Business firms hire management consultants to come in and examine their operations, not because the consultants are more intelligent or more mature, but because they are from outside and so can see things in balance and perspective. Youth have a similar function in the church. I want you to stay with me in the place where you can share them. As a fellow Christian I need you and I think there are a lot of others who need you too."

Adolescents have different ways of expressing their doubt about the church and their unsureness about God. They can be defiant ("I refuse to go to that hypocrite-filled church any more"); they can be convincingly reasonable ("I don't think I'll go to church today; I've got too much homework and I know you want me on the honor roll"); sometimes they are provocative ("What do you get out of going to church? Do you think it really makes any difference?").

But behind all of this is a coming of age in faith. There is an insistent voice within youth that is saying: "God can no longer be taken for granted. It is not enough for me to assume my parents' attitudes toward God or slip into my parents' practices in the church. What happens from now on must be *mine.*"

What the parents must know (regardless of how they choose to respond to it) is that this doubt and questioning and rebellion is evidence that something deeply significant is taking place in the personality of their offspring. Their teenagers are wondering what it is going to be like to maintain adult relationships with God. They are making the preparatory moves in coming to their own adult, personal faith in Christ. It should be counted as a good time (if not a smooth time) because the parents can now share the struggles and achievements of their own Christian faith with these emerging persons. Resistance to the church is not the first step to atheism—it is more likely to be a natural development in discipleship.

If parents will not permit the possibility of dissent they also prevent the possibility of a free yes. If parents refuse to listen to the sounds of rebellion and the stuttering of doubt they will only cut themselves off from being in on the very interesting process by which a person learns how to make the decisions of faith.

It is important for Christian parents to formulate for themselves a goal in relation to their children's faith in God. Do we want them to grow up and rubber-stamp what we have taught them, unchanged and unchallenged? Or do we want them, with curiosity and questing, to deal with all that has been given, discovering the personal dimension of a new life in Christ for themselves? If it is the latter, we must remember that there is much that our children see in us that is less than the best and which should be rejected. There is also much in the church that is wrong and needs correction. We need to remember, too, that we do not know the exact form the Christian experience will take, even in our own children. This new person in Christ that we pray our child will be is a fresh, new creation of God, not the result of our genes and teaching, but the result of God's call and challenge.

Parents who prefer the kind of people who have never examined the meaning of their life in relation to the call of God are going to think that when that examination does begin to take place there is a "youth" problem or a "religious" problem. Others will know that the Christian gospel has at its center a plea for personal decisions. "No inherited religion," it says; "your faith has to be your own, not your father's." And these parents, when the adolescent in their home begins to resist the church, will be ready to give thanks to God that yet another person is beginning to sense the personal dimensions of a relationship with God, and realize that the saying of no is the first step in discovering how to say yes. (It may help to remember that we went through a very similar process when our children were two and three years old—the difference now is that God not the parent is "the opposition.") Parents can hardly prefer that a child blandly and impersonally continue in a stream of institutional religion, inheriting faith third-hand: they will want a free, adult relationship with Christ.

Parents acquire the wisdom to deal with the actual details involved in these matters when they ask God for the grace to be honest, open, and faithful to youth; that they be given the resilience, the strength, and grace to engage in frank conversation about their own life in Christ; that they be kept from bluffing; that they be prevented from letting their own pride interfere in the development of this new person in Christ; and that their lives will be deepened and enriched through sharing the development in Christ of this newly emerging person in their home.

3 "You Can't Make Me!"

Adolescence is a time of challenge to parental authority. That the parents *have* authority is obvious. How they exercise that authority is not. Under the defiance and questioning and pressure of adolescent rebellion, parents are forced to examine the base of their authority and to evaluate the ways in which they choose to exercise it.

* * * * * * *

1. In what ways did you rebel against the authority of your parents? What forms did your rebellion take? How did your parents respond to your rebellion?

2. In what ways do your teenagers express rebellion? What are the key issues in your home around which conflict with authority takes place?

3. How do you feel when your parental authority is defied? What do you do?

4. Read Luke 2:41-51. What tensions do you notice here in the relationship between parental authority and adolescent rebellion?

5. What are your models for exercising authority? Figures from your family? Persons in history? Biblical personalities?

6. Discuss this statement by Lionel Whiston: "A dictator in a home or in a nation chooses the way of quick returns .... There can be a subtle parental pride in exacting obedience, much like bringing a dog to heel. 'Good' children can be displayed, to the parents' advantage."[1]

* * * * * * *

Challenges to parental authority—a commonplace in adolescence —cannot be settled simply by quoting St. Paul, "Children, obey your parents in the Lord, for this is right." Adolescents are quite likely to have read the letter to the Ephesians, too, and able to do some quoting of their own: "Fathers, do not provoke your children to anger, but bring them up in the discipline and instruction of the Lord." (Ephesians 6:1,4)

If one of the essential tasks of adolescence is to learn to internalize acts of obedience and submission, to learn how to be instructed and guided and led by the elders, the corresponding task of parenthood is to learn how to exercise the authority in proper ways, in wise ways, in Christian ways.

I have little patience, I must confess, with those parental bull-sessions which trade opinions on how to make the children behave, and lament the sad straits our society is in because of the young who have no respect for authority. They would do much better to discuss the ways in which they themselves exercise authority, just how they acquired the authority they do have, and under what conditions they can retain it. There is a clear Biblical mandate that parents exercise authority and that children subject themselves to it. But there is also a Biblical context in which it is to be done—a style and a grace—and parents need to pay particular attention to that.

Given this general structure, that parents have authority and children are required to obey, the question that parents with adolescents need to answer is not, "How do I get my child to obey me?" but, "How can I properly and wisely exercise my authority?"

And that is a shift: for it was the other way around during the years of childhood. Then the parental task was to teach the child obedience. But once the child reaches adolescence the parents must spend much more time and attention on the way they exercise authority, and correspondingly less on worrying whether obedience is forthcoming.

I am always a little puzzled by the preference some parents have for Proverbs 13:24 ("he who spares the rod hates his son") over Luke 2:41-51 (the twelve-year-old Jesus at the temple) as a model for the exercise of authority. Not that they do not both give good guidance, but the proverb is a condensed, pungent admonition that the parent take seriously the task of discipline, while the story gives an actual example of how it was done in the family of Joseph and Mary when Jesus was an adolescent. What I suspect (maybe I am unkind) is that some parents want a Biblical excuse to beat children who do not do what they are told, and are impatient with any counsel which involves them as parents in a process of growth along with their

children. The proverb can, by isolating it, be used as a slogan justify-
ing corporal punishment; the story cannot be used as a slogan for
anything—it can only draw the parent into the ambiguities of
parenthood and give a deeper sensitivity to the anxieties and uncertainties in which parenthood involves us.

It was no easier for Joseph and Mary to be parents of an adolescent than it is for any of the rest of us. The Passover experience in
Jerusalem during Jesus' twelfth year shows the tensions that develop between authority and obedience in even the best of homes.
The family had, presumably, made the annual Passover pilgrimage
from Nazareth to Jerusalem many times. After the festival and on
their return, a day's journey out of Jerusalem, the parents discovered that their son was not with them. Anxious and fearful they
returned to the city to search for him. They found him "in the
temple, sitting among the teachers, listening to them and asking
them questions." Then the confrontation between parent and
youth: " 'Son, why have you treated us so? Behold, your father and
I have been looking for you anxiously.' " In Mary's eyes Jesus had
been both disobedient and inconsiderate. The parental authority
had not been honored. Without their knowledge and against their
will he had remained in the temple. If the question is to be narrowed
to a question of authority and obedience the story must stop right
there: Mary and Joseph are right; Jesus is wrong. Period. If all
guidance were restricted to Proverbs 13:24 Joseph would have taken
off his belt, administered a good whipping in front of the rabbis, and
taken his son back to Nazareth. But Luke doesn't see it that way.
He continues the story with Jesus' words, " 'How is it that you
sought me? Did you not know that I must be in my Father's
house?' " "Why," in other words, "are you trying to control every
move I make? That was all right when I was small, but I am no
longer the child whom you had to watch all the time. I have a life
apart from you—my relation to God is going to take me into ways
you cannot anticipate. I am going to be moving beyond the realm
of your expectations. There are requirements in my life that you do
not place upon me. There is more to my life than just doing what
you say—I am beginning to feel additional obligations. The world
is more than home and worship in Nazareth—I am beginning to
live in the wider world of 'my Father's house.' I came to the temple

in obedience to you—do you not see that the obedience begun in response to you must continue apart from you?"

The adolescent is more than the sum total of what the mother and the father have produced. The parent, as representative of God's guidance, must be ready to step aside when the time comes. The adolescent presents parents with a reality that they cannot manage or control: a new person, in process of becoming an adult person, is aborning. Jesus rejects his mother's reprimand and stresses his own personal needs and God's authority over him. He implies that it involves more of a world than the parents are aware of. The divine command first heard through the mediation of parental authority can have shape and force apart from parental commands.

"And he went down with them and came to Nazareth, and was obedient to them; and his mother kept all these things in her heart." The parents continued to exercise authority; the young man still submitted in obedience. But from this time on there was a difference. Never again could obedience be interpreted as living up to the letter of parental expectations, although these could not be ignored. The reciprocities of authority and obedience were still in operation, but the context was wider.

The story is gentle, quiet, reflective. There is no counsel here for parents who want to "keep their kids in line." There is no license for youth to "do whatever they feel." There is a breaking out of parent-child molds and a model of flexibility which is aware of new reality from the point of view of both parent and youth.

There are several words in the Hebrew language for a child, each describing a different aspect of level of growth. Two of the more descriptive are *taph*, in popular etymology, a child clinging to its mother; and *naar*, in popular etymology, one who shakes himself free. Jesus in the temple had just made the transition from *taph* to *naar*. And Joseph and Mary were intelligent enough to notice: they did not insist on exercising their parental authority in the ways that had worked before; they did not try to force the *naar* back into the mold of the *taph*. They adapted their parental style to the new reality of *naar*. They did not relinquish parental authority, but exercised it differently.

No one can write a handbook on how to negotiate the shifting requirements of authority and obedience during the adolescent years. But there are some insights that emerge from Luke's passage that provide useful wisdom. The first is that authority when challenged should not bluster. William James wrote: "I am done with Great things and Big things, with Great institutions and Big success, and I am for those tiny invisible molecular forces, that work from individual to individual, creeping through the crannies of the world like so many soft rootlets, or like the capillary oozing of water, but which, give them time, will rend the hardest monuments of men's pride." The statement provides a perspective for the exercise of parental authority in relation to the adolescent. Parental authority does not gain in strength as the voice is raised or the punishments increased. If as the child gets bigger the "stick" also gets bigger, the parents most certainly have a mistaken idea of their authority and how to exercise it. Mary and Joseph took the route of quiet counsel, patient trust, pondering and praying.

A second insight is that authority must be courteous. There was no pushing, shoving, or yelling in that temple scene. Just because parents have a Biblical basis for exercising authority does not mean that they are exempt from the common courtesies as they do it. Exercising authority does not mean doing whatever you wish however you wish. A line in George Eliot's *Middlemarch* describes some parents: ". . . persons whose celestial intimacies seemed not to improve their domestic manners."[2] The fifth Commandment is not divine sanction for parents to enforce arbitrary and selfish whims on their children; it is a gift to assist them in rearing children to God. Parents are warned not to take advantage of it for their own convenience: "He who troubles his household will inherit the wind." (Proverbs 11:29) Very often parents use the authority God gave them as a license to get their own way, completely ignoring the fact that their authority is for the purpose of "discipline and instruction in the Lord." That is a serious lapse of responsibility on the parents' part. Parents will be attuned to the basic courtesies surrounding authority if they will look at their children as a father did in a John Updike short story, "not as our creations but our guests, people who enter the world by our invitation. . . ."[3]

A third insight is that authority is not coercive. Since parental authority is conferred by God, our "Lord and King," it should be used, insofar as that is possible for us, in a godlike manner. How *does* God exercise his authority? Plainly, not with a heavy hand. He does not coerce. As one early church father put it, "Force is no attribute of God." God is not a bully. He is not a despot. He does not push his children around. He creates us, provides for us, loves us, and disciplines us: but he does not *make* us do anything. There are corrections and punishments, patient instruction and clear example, the disciplines of history and circumstance, but he does not force his will upon us. That pattern is so overwhelmingly clear in Scripture that there is no excuse for any parents to assume divine authority for acting as dictators to their offspring. The same God who gives parents authority over their children also demonstrates how the authority is to be used.

It is quite true that when our children are small it is necessary, at times, to force our will upon them and make them do something they do not want to do: we forcibly snatch them out of the path of a speeding automobile, we make them take a medicine that tastes awful, we insist that they go to school when they would rather play with a new electric train. But in the long perspective of growing up these are exceptions. It is simply a mistake to extrapolate from such instances to the world of the adolescent and claim that since we are wiser, more experienced, and more knowledgeable about the world we must make them do what we want them to do. The fact is that we can't. We are no longer strong enough, present enough, or smart enough to do it. But neither should we. Authority loses its moral force and spiritual energy when it becomes authoritarian.

It is well to remember that the majority of men have never invented the device of beating children into submission. . . . The device of beating children down—by superior force, by contrived logic, or by vicious sweetness—makes it unnecessary for the adult to become adult. He need not develop that true inner superiority which is naturally persuasive. Instead, he is authorized to remain significantly inconsistent and arbitrary, or in other words, childish, while beating into the child the desirability of growing up. The child, forced out of fear to pretend that he is better when seen than when unseen, is left to anticipate the day when he will have the brute power to make others more moral than he ever intends to be himself.

Erik Erikson[4]

The words which typically describe God's way of exercising authority among his people are *musar* (in Hebrew) and *paideia* (in Greek). The usual translation in English Bibles is "discipline." Unfortunately, the word seems to have been reduced to something equivalent to punishment. "Do you discipline your child?" in colloquial speech usually means, "Do you spank him when he's naughty?" If the word is to be used at all it must be used with its original content: training and instruction. The disciplinarian is not one who follows people around in order to catch them in an error and then administer forty lashes of punishment "to teach them not to do it again." Closer to the core of the meaning of the word is the image of the master craftsman who takes to himself an apprentice: over a period of years he offers himself as a model, provides guidelines, gives encouragement, points out errors, demonstrates skill, establishes standards, rejects sloppy or careless work. The discipline involves a personal association which makes it possible for the younger to be shaped by the maturity of the older. The heart of discipline, and the most Biblical expression of authority, is careful attention which guides growth.

4 "You Wouldn't Understand!"

Adolescence is full of misunderstandings. Youth find it difficult to express what they feel and what they think, and frequently blame others for the breakdown in communications. They often conclude that the parent generation is not capable of understanding the youth experience. Parents who do not accept the conclusion must do more than argue against it; they must provide actual evidence to counteract it.

* * * * * * *

1. When you have something you want to share and to talk over, who do you go to? Who is your favorite conversationalist? What is it that makes that person easy to converse with?
2. What are the usual topics of conversation between you and your teenager? What topics are not discussed at all, or, at the most, infrequently?
3. Do you ever plan conversations with your adolescent? Or do they just grow out of the routines of the household?
4. Note the distinctions between the generations in Joel 2:28 and 1 John 2:13. What is attributed to each generation?
5. What realities in your life do you think your child is not likely to understand, or even be interested in understanding?
6. What new listening skills have you acquired in the last few years? Do you use them as well within your family as you do outside it?
7. What realities in your child's life seem very remote from you? —things with which you have had very little recent experience or interest?

* * * * * * *

Youth often claim to be misunderstood. They *are* often misunderstood—I am sympathetic to the complaint and try to do something about it. But sometimes they (or others, supposed to be their advocates) try to elevate the experience of misunderstanding into a dogma—that there can be no converse between the generations, that elders are incapable of listening to youth, that youth experience only futility when they seek to speak to adults. That is not only wrong, but silly. The experience of misunderstanding needs to be faced by parents with careful attention, but the dogma of the "gap" can be brushed aside as a fabrication by fools.

We live in an age when it is widely supposed that communication is a matter of technics: that the telephone, the radio, the television and other electronic devices make it possible for people to say things to each other accurately and listen to each other understandingly. But there is no evidence for it. Electronics makes it possible for us to speak over long distances, and it makes it possible to speak to many people at once, but, so far anyway, it has not increased our power for either saying things more accurately or listening to them more attentively. A word does not gain in meaning when it is amplified; nor does a sentence become clearer when it is heard by a million people instead of just one. If there is going to be improved communication between parents and youth it will come as they acquire more skill in having something to say and learning how to listen, not in turning up the volume of the transistor or buying a larger stereo.

There are, of course, differences between the generations, and the differences do contribute to misunderstandings: words are used differently, assumptions are diverse, interests are not the same, needs are not the same. But the differences, while making some misunderstanding certain, also make good communication possible, for because of the differences there is something worth saying, something the other does not know, something that parents would not come up with on their own or youth discover by themselves. Addressing a similar problem, except he was talking about conversations across the centuries, not just generations, Newman very wisely noted: "Even mistakes carry information; for they are cognate to the truth, and we can allow for them."[1]

Some gaps are undesirable. A gap between the window and its frame through which windy gusts of winter air can penetrate is not good. A gap that widens in a cracked sidewalk is a hazard—a place to catch people's toes and cause them to stumble and fall. But other kinds of gaps are good. In spark plugs, for instance. The action part of the spark plug is a gap in an electrical circuit. Electricity flows across this gap and creates a spark which ignites the gasoline in an internal combustion engine. If the gap is eliminated, there is no spark, and no ignition. The difference between the parent and youth generations is a gap of this kind. Far from being an aberration which needs to be repaired, it is a design to be preserved.

There is no question that inter-generational conversation is more difficult than the kind we engage in with a few friends we have known half our lives. But many important things are difficult. The unwillingness of both parents and youth to make the effort to speak across generation barriers has resulted in what Lewis Mumford decries as "the dire insufficiencies of current one-generation knowledge."[2]

In one of his letters, St. John made a sharp distinction between parents and youth: "I write to you who are now *fathers*, because you have known him who has always existed. And to you vigorous *young men* I am writing because you have been strong in defeating the evil one." (1 John 2:13, Phillips, italics mine) The parent generation and the youth generation, in St. John's mind, were different, having different needs and different strengths. The prophet Joel also distinguished between the generations when he said, "your old men shall dream dreams, and your young men shall see visions." (Joel 2:28)

Not only are there generation differences, but it is God's will that they be there. The younger and older generations have special contributions to make to each other. If the differences were eliminated there would be nothing to exchange. If the gap were closed there would be no "spark" to ignite vast areas of experience. Once parents are convinced that the generation gap is a good thing, part of God's creative design, they will find ways to use it as a stimulus to better conversation. They will give up attempts at homogenizing the generations, knowing that will only produce a dull and colorless (and un-Biblical) result. And they will refuse to contribute to popular gossip on the "generation gap."

If communication difficulties between parents and youth are going to be turned to good use, parents need to understand and develop their strengths, their "differences," so they will have something to share when the opportunity arises. It is unfortunate when parents, not realizing the necessity for difference, attempt to deny

their "older-generation" status by talking, dressing, and acting con-
spicuously in the style of youth. Parental use of youth fashions, hip
talk, and consumer habits say to youth, "I don't accept my position
as a member of my own generation. I don't like it. I don't find any
meaning or sense in it."

It is also unfortunate when parents abdicate their generation
position by self-deprecation, disclaiming wisdom or useful experience: "oh my, things are *so* different today. I really don't know what
I would do if I had to be a young person again. Things are just so
horribly confusing with the pill and the Bomb and all." This con-
stitutes a withdrawal from relationship. Parents who react this
way disqualify themselves from *meaning* anything to the younger
generation.

And it is unfortunate when parents misuse their generation status
by aggressively assaulting youth with bluster and pontification:
"When you have a few more years on you, my boy, you will feel a
lot differently, I assure you." If the parent generation supposes that
its major contribution across the gap must be in the form of advice-
giving they will pretty quickly foul the plugs. Only if advice is the
natural overflow of an acquired, living strength and Christian purpose will it be of any use.

On the other hand, when the parent generation develops a robust
pride in its position, that is fortunate. God has chosen to place some
persons at this particular place in time and history in the parent
generation. There can be a firm commitment to the calling of what
it means to be an adult in relation to youth, a parent in relation to
son and daughter.

One area in which the parent generation has a unique contribution to make is in the achievement of intimacy—closeness. Intimacy
is the capacity to share yourself with another person completely.
Parents have the strength of intimacy. When you are unsure of
yourself you don't dare share yourself. If you do, you risk rejection
and wounding. Youth are usually not sure of themselves and,
though they long for it, they are not good at intimacy. They are not
confident enough of themselves to venture out. Too many fears rise
up: "What if the other person refuses my love, or my friendship, or
my help; might that not mean that I am not worth loving, or not
needed as a friend, or not useful as a helper?" But adults, some of

them anyway, have weathered these self-doubts and have experienced a venturing of themselves into the no-man's-land of other people's hearts. When you are strong you can afford to be vulnerable. The parent generation has the obligation first to achieve and then to demonstrate this intimacy—to show that it is possible and to show what it looks like.

Another parent-generation strength is the ability to care. The capacity to relate to another person in a caring way is an achievement of maturity. Youth have moments when they care, but it is not characteristic among them to have the sustained strength and the emotional stability for the faithful caring of another. That is a skill that the older generation teaches by demonstration. You don't learn to be a caring *person* the same way you learn to care for a pet: by threats, work-charts and reward-oriented performance ("you can watch TV an extra hour tonight if you walk the dog"). You learn to care by being cared for. The parent generation, simply by doing a good job of caring, puts the younger generation into a position of care-apprenticeship. By being linked generationally to a caring person, youth not only derive the benefit of being cared for but also pick up skill in caring on their own.

The positive qualities accessible to the parent generation can be clarified and accented. An exercise in list-making, itemizing characteristics and gifts discoverable within the least of us, frequently uncovers a surprising number of things that spark love and hope across the generation gap. The self-doubts that many adults have concerning their own legitimacy lead some into an enormous vindictiveness toward the young. The self-confidence that it is possible for the Christian to affirm in Christ can convert those negative relations into intelligent and courteous conversations that develop mature love.

The youth generation has its own responsibilities in doing something about communication misunderstandings, but that is not in focus here. They need to learn to be honest with their own lives and responsible to the task of being obedient to God in *their* generation —to "be strong in defeating the evil one," as St. John wrote, and to "see visions," as Joel wrote. The parent generation, meanwhile, needs to accept its primary responsibility, fulfilling its own tasks, and not complain about what the other generation is or is not doing.

There is a strong sense of rivalry and competition between the generations which can be used either creatively or destructively. Youth, perhaps, feel it more keenly than adults. This competitive impulse often leads to tactics that are designed to defeat an enemy rather than to share a strength. Youth want to win. One technique of battle is propaganda: convince your opponents that they are not worthy, not good enough, to be on the same field with you. Demoralize your enemy and you might not have to fight them.

So if youth say, "Don't trust anyone over thirty" they are not saying it on the basis of a careful sociological survey of people over thirty. They are engaging in propaganda. They are saying, "Integrity and trust are essential to human experience. The one who has them deserves the leadership. I want the leadership. And I am more qualified—after all, everyone knows that you can't trust anyone over thirty." If no one examines the hidden parts of the argument, youth just might get away with it. It is essentially a bragging statement that distracts attention from the braggart by concentrating on the claimed defects of the opponent.

The basic rule for parents is "Don't let the opposition define your position, and make sure you know your own." Young people are good at many things; they are valuable for many things. But they are not good at evaluating the parent generation, nor should parents be surprised when they are not.

In a world where differences frequently degenerate into conflicts, the parent generation must take the lead in showing that generation differences are opportunities for an exchange of personal love, faith, and hope—not occasions to seek an advantage or assert a superiority. But even when conflict threatens there should be no attempt to obscure or suppress the differences. There is a great temptation at such times to blur differences under the impulse of momentary good fellowship, which substitutes passing goodwill for mature love. There is, also, the more brutal suppression of difference by forcing conformity. But besides being immoral, a fascist technique, it is unworkable.

The parent can acquire the perspective, the experience, and the Biblical insight to accept the generation differences as an opportunity for lively conversational exchanges of affection, admiration, wisdom, excitement, dreams and visions, knowledge and victories.

The presence of differences always heightens the enjoyments of love. Differences in the beloved cause unending surprise, interest, and joy. If the younger (or older) generation was perfectly conformable to the expectations of the other, the capacities for love would diminish and experiences of joy would flatten.

Wise parents guard and celebrate generational differences. They know they have gifts to share—and are sure that there are gifts among the youth they will receive with benefit. They are open to the exchange of old men's dreams and young men's visions which are featured in every new movement of the Holy Spirit and often have their origin in a conversation.

"You Never
5 Trust Me!"

At no other time in life does a person experience more insecurity than during adolescence. The adolescent is erratic and inconsistent. Character is in process of being formed but it is far from finished. The terrific insecurity produces a great need to trust and be trusted. The parent is in a key position to contribute an experience of basic trust during this period.

* * * * * * *

1. What are the uncertainties and insecurities that you imagine are going on in youth? Spend some time trying to get inside their feelings. Can you remember some of yours when you were an adolescent?

2. What kind of trust relationship do you have with your children? In what areas do you trust them? In what areas do you not trust them? How do you express your trust? Your mistrust?

3. What insecurities do you face at this time in your life? Are they related mostly to health, job, death, children, or other areas? How does your trust in the faithfulness of God provide direction for growth?

4. What kind of trust relationship do you have with God? Do you trust him? Does he trust you? How do you show your trust for him? How does he treat you?

5. Psalm 91 expresses a sense of trust in God. Read it and discuss the ingredients of trust: What experiences does this psalmist have which result in trust?

6. The experience of being trusted, and a character of trustworthiness, go hand in hand. What things do you do to encourage and develop them in your child?

* * * * * * *

Here is a scenario for mistrust between parent and youth. The setting is routine Americana: a family room littered with records, some empty coke bottles, and a thoroughly unkempt teenager. It is late Saturday morning—say eleven o'clock—when the father, cleanly shaven, carrying himself with the assurance of a man who has gotten and is getting things done, walks briskly through the room. The dialogue is an old summer rerun.

Youth: Say, Dad, some of the gang are going to the Millers' cabin up in the woods for the weekend. I think I'll join them. OK?

Parent: Nope! Who knows what you'd get into up there.

Youth: You never trust me! I ask for permission to do the most innocent things, and you imagine some kind of stinking orgy!

Parent: You bet your life I don't trust you. I asked you to have the car in last night by midnight and when did you pull in?—two o'clock in the morning. You told me you'd have the lawn mowed by Wednesday and look at it—it's a wonder the neighbors haven't gotten together and bought us a goat. You start showing me I can trust you, and I'll trust you all right.

As the day goes on, the moods of both harden into anger, resentment, and suspicion. The father looks at his son as a bundle of erratic impulses, ill-controlled desires, and selfish demands. The son looks at the father as a rigid dictator, obsessed with getting things done, no matter how trivial they might be, and an expert at anticipating the opinion of the neighbors on a wide range of subjects, but less than interested in what his own child might feel or think.

Meanwhile trust between parent and youth has disappeared without leaving a trace. Both are thinking the worst of each other, and then projecting these thoughts and feelings into the future of their relationship. For an outsider to encourage either of them to trust would seem to be naive. After all, doesn't each have good reason to mistrust the other?

The frequency, even the inevitability, of this unhappy exchange doesn't make it any less a disaster. When things happen often, no matter how bad they are, we succumb to a kind of psychic numbing—we cease to *feel* the awfulness. One death is a personal tragedy; a million deaths is a statistical item in a history book. Loss of trust in the family is so frequent today that it is no more than a statistic for many. If it is happening to everyone else, we think, it must be like the common cold—put up with it, complain as little as possible, and quit wasting time looking for a cure.

But no parent—least of all a Christian parent—has to dumbly acquiesce to this death of trust in the family. Anyone tricked into accepting it simply because of its high incidence is being robbed of the advantages that the Christian gospel brings into family life. The life of Christ has insights and energies to transform and sustain family life. According to Howard Clinebell, parents are the " 'architects of the family' ";[1] they are in a position and have the power to re-shape the atmosphere and re-establish the trust.

Christian parents are both teachers and learners of trust. They are teachers of trust as parents. They are learners of trust as persons —and their personhood has a new birth in the Christian faith.

The teaching of trust that took place when the youth was an infant is still accessible to a parent's memory. As the infant grew, there were many experiences that threw open the whole question of whether the infant would trust or mistrust. The world was hard, intractable, unresponsive. Floors were cold, meals were tardy, movements were uncoordinated, strange faces appeared in blurred focus. But the faithful, consistent, affectionate presence of the parent finally succeed in instilling a sense of basic trust in children, a sense that the world and the people in it are *for* them, that their basic needs have a good chance of being satisfied, that obstacles can be overcome, that they themselves are worth something and can accomplish things.

The results of instilling a basic trust in a child surface in the standard episode of learning how to walk. When children begin venturing into an upright position, and taking a few uncertain steps, they fall down. Sometimes they hurt themselves. When that happens, the parents don't scold or spank them. They don't say, "Aha, I knew you wouldn't be able to walk; I told you so." They know that learning to walk takes a lot of practice; that there is a lot of unsuccessful trying that goes into making the achievement. If a child is whipped or scolded every time it falls, the child will probably quit trying. It would be much easier to crawl—less trouble, safer, and certainly a lot less punishment.

While not enjoying the spectacle of their children falling and hurting themselves as they learn to walk, parents persist in encouraging them to keep trying. They keep saying (countering the actual experience of the child), "I'm sure you can do it; keep trying."

But how are the parents so sure? They certainly have no proof from performance. They are sure because they trust the capacity for growth and development in their child. They know that other persons have been through it and succeeded. They know that they themselves have been through the process.

Youth learn to be trusted (and to trust) much the same way they learn to walk, not by first demonstrating it as an achievement, but by being encouraged, supported, and assured by those who have been through it themselves. The parental support is critical. If there is only a punishing, blaming, mistrusting reaction when youth show themselves to be untrustworthy, they will scarcely have the courage to develop those capacities and strengths that are worthy of trust.

If the parents refuse to trust until their children prove that they are worthy of being trusted, trust simply will not develop. All adolescents are, at various times and places, untrustworthy. There is no mystery behind that: they have drives, impulses, ideas, and dreams crashing around in a new mind and body with still undeveloped controls. They are naturally going to do things that betray and disappoint parental trust. They are going to fail. Failure is one of the great, pervasive experiences of adolescence. A failure to prove trustworthy is not the least of the failures.

The great differential among adolescents comes, not from degrees of their trustworthiness, but from how their failures in trust are treated by others. They only learn to be trustworthy by being trusted. Are the parents willing to risk and suffer ventures into trust? Are they willing to exercise the same patience and hope with the spiritual character of their teenager as they did with the physical body of their infant?

Christian parents gather even deeper insights into the dynamics of trust when they consider how they themselves have been treated by God. As parents of children, they have taught trust; as Christians, they have learned it, and learned it in such a personal way that they are especially well equipped to deal with the stresses that afflict trust during the youth years.

We are told repeatedly in Scripture to "trust God." We are asked to assume confidently that he will work in us and in the world powerfully and victoriously. But who can engage in such trust?

Elaborate arguments about the power of God and the love of God, even if they are stated with the most forceful logic, never seem to be the key to initiating a person into the actual experience of trusting God. What we do see happen is that people trust God when they experience in a personal way God's treatment of them. They find that even though they are unacceptable, God through Christ accepts them. "God shows his love for us in that while we were yet sinners Christ died for us." (Romans 5:8) God calls us; we answer. God forgives us; we accept his forgiveness. God acts toward us in a way which draws forth our trust; and we trust him.

In matters that are at the very core of our existence, we learn through demonstration, by having truth done to and for us. God demonstrated in Jesus Christ. He did it first, to make it possible for us to do it. "We love, because he first loved us" is the way St. John put it (1 John 4:19). Christians learn to trust God not because they have been convinced by arguments that they should trust him but because they have been treated by God in a loving, accepting, trusting way *before* they were lovable, acceptable, or trustworthy.

And that is the thing that all Christians have in common—a basic trust in God. It is extremely important to keep in mind how we got it, how we came to the point of trusting God ourselves. It is quite obvious we didn't come to it by being scolded or bullied or argued into it. We learned to trust, because we experienced God in Christ acting toward us in such a way that he made it possible for us to trust. We learned to trust by being trusted.

That is the experience that equips parents to demonstrate and to share trust with their adolescent child. During the years when trust is subject to so many tensions and dislocations, during the episodes when there is simply no objective reason for engaging in trust, that God-human experience of trust is a standing reminder of how trust is learned. No matter how many times our children betray trust, no matter how undeserving they are of it, no matter what burdens are placed upon it by the imperfect love between parent and youth, trust can always be restored and established. God's way of establishing and developing trust in his children is to make the first move, to give a demonstration of what he means by it. That continues to be the best model for Christian parents who want to build trust in their family.

Many parents have learned to respond to their teenager's "You never trust me" with something like this: "I know it must seem like that to you. And I admit it's a real problem I have. But let's not say 'never.' I have trusted you a great deal in the past, and I'm going to do it a lot more in the future. It's more a case, isn't it, of learning to trust each other? The main thing in life for me is trusting God —really living in trusting dependence on his grace. Faith, I guess, is the best word for it. I'm no expert at it as you well know, but I'm trying. And as I'm trying, I'm finding that life is very, very different. As I develop in my basic trust in God, there is a spillover into my relations with other people: I know that God loves them and is working in them as well as in me. Instead of looking for the worst in them, examining them to find out their sins, I keep expecting to find some evidence of God's love operating in them. And I find myself trusting more and more.

"I think you and I can do that with each other more than we have. As we trust God, we can expect that trust to spill over into our feelings and expectations for each other. Neither of us is quite trustworthy, you know, when it comes down to a detailed examination. But the God who lives and works in us is. Being quite sure of that, we can grow in our trust of each other."

"If You Loved Me, You'd Let Me!"

6

The experience of love, which is basic between parent and child, is thrown into disarray during adolescence. The kinds of love which worked and were satisfying, both from parent to child and from child to parent, no longer work and are no longer satisfying. In the confusion love itself is called into question—both sides doubt the other's love. And rightly, for the old loves are no longer adequate for the new reality.

* * * * * * * *

1. Has your child ever said, "I hate you" or at least words to that effect? What circumstances provoked the outburst? Do you think the words were meant? What experience, what feeling do you think is behind the words?

2. Have you ever said, or felt like saying, to your teenager, "I hate you—I'm fed up with you—I've had it with you"? Describe the circumstances around one of these episodes. What experience and feeling is behind your words?

3. Differentiate the ways in which you love: your spouse, your pet, your hobby, your best friend, your children, your parents, your job. Be as precise as you can in understanding how each of these can be "love" while each involves different content.

4. Discuss the ways in which your love has developed and grown. How is your love of your spouse now different from the "first love" you had as a young person? How is your love of your parents now different from what it was when you were six years old? How is your love of your teenager different from that same person when an infant?

5. Read 1 Corinthians 13. What in these words seems to you important for prodding and shaping a growth in the love you have for your son or daughter?

* * * * * * * *

Any parents who have lived for twelve to sixteen years with a child "love" that child. There can hardly be any question about that. They feel it in their bones. They have a rich accumulation of experience to document the strength of that love. There have been long sleepless nights spent nursing an illness, panicked trips to the hospital following an accident, patient hours listening as a young mind grappled with the mysteries of words and numbers, silent restrained suffering as innocent little people encountered the baffling perplexities of new schools and neighborhoods. All this and more the parents have experienced as forms of love. And the love has not been without its rewards. During the early years affection found a focus in the infant, and the senses found gratification in acts of fathering and mothering. As the child grew, there was the satisfaction of being needed, of knowing that you are worth something, that your care, your guidance, your protection were necessary. There were shared pleasures of discovery, of learning, of affection. The child brightened what might have been very lonely hours; the child gave meaning to what in other circumstances might have been very onerous tasks. However selfless in its motivation, parental love is invariably rich in reward. In some ways there is no love which is quite so surrounded with pleasures over so wide a range of experience as the love of parent for a child.

But adolescence interrupts these patterns of love that have been developed, usually quite satisfactorily, through the years of childhood. However, the interruption is not accomplished with a clean re-definition: it is uneven, unsystematic, and confused. The parents cannot understand why the way they have expressed love for so long does not work any more. The youth cannot understand why the way they have experienced love for so long no longer satisfies.

In frustration youth scream, "If you loved me, you'd let me do what I want!" The parents are forced to a self-examination: "If I love him adequately, why is he so unhappy; why doesn't my love bring its old results?" The main experience youth have had with love up to this point is that it has fulfilled their needs. Parental love has been a love which satisfied them. Not that it was recklessly indulgent—there would have been the usual limits and the customary no's—but on the whole the dominant experience would be a love which provided satisfaction for basic needs. But in adolescence other needs are added—the need to express oneself, the need to "be myself," the need to make personal decisions, the need to exercise will power. The parent cannot satisfy those needs in the same way that childhood needs were satisfied—by providing, by comforting, by anticipating and planning, by understanding. In fact, the parent cannot satisfy those needs at all. So the youth, who is used to having needs satisfied by parental love, and the parents, who are used to seeing their love make a difference to their child, are both unhappy.

Christian parents have a particularly sharp advantage over those outside the Christian tradition in finding a way out of this dilemma. The Christian faith has been exceptionally fortunate in having theologians and scholars who have pondered and reflected on the enormous complexity of the experience that is lumped together under the category "love," have brought clarity to the jumble, and provide guidance to the perplexed.

The theological tradition of the church has distinguished four kinds of love. The distinctions are a boon to parents who seek an orientation in the mix-up they experience in loving their children.

The first of the loves is simple affection. It is the most natural of the loves. It is a love which happens to us whether we do anything or not. It grows up as a seemingly natural part of life. It gives itself no airs, makes no claims, needs no promises. We do not ask if something or someone is worthy of our affection—we feel affection simply because we feel it. One Greek lexicon defines it as "affection, especially of parents to offspring." C. S. Lewis, who distinguishes between Need-love and Gift-love, finds them interrelated in this love a parent has for a child: "The Need and the Need-love of the young is obvious; so is the Gift-love of the mother. She gives birth, gives suck, gives protection. On the other hand, she must give birth or die. She must give suck or suffer. That way, her Affection too is a Need-love. There is the paradox. It is a Need-love but what it needs is to give. It is a Gift-love but it needs to be needed."[1]

At adolescence, though, this admirable gift-need symbiosis comes to an end. No longer does the youth need love in quite the same ways, no longer is the parent capable of giving love in the same forms. There are still needs to be met on the part of youth, and there are still gifts to share on the part of the parent, but they do not so neatly intermesh. Both find that their needs are no longer being met by the other—although the youth are usually the first to announce it.

Next there is the love which is friendship. It is based on common interest and shared experience. It involves companionship and conversation. Workers often find it as they pour energy into a common task; athletes sometimes find it as they engage, alternately, in the competition and cooperation that games involve. It is essentially a relationship between peers. It insists on mutuality. Each has something to give and something to receive from the other. Each respects the other and honors the other. There can be no friendship between the weak and the strong, between the slave and the free, between the rich and the poor. Unless, of course, those designations are incidental to something which is discovered between two people that is more basic and obliterates the conventional labels. It would seem that this love is not possible between parent and child where one has so much to give and the other so much to receive. But it occurs nevertheless. It occurs at the moments when parents fantasize themselves into the world of childhood, pretending to be in the world of toy soldiers and immersing themselves in the delights of faerie—at those moments friendship is experienced. There are corresponding moments when the child in fantasy lives as an adult and becomes a companion in the regular work world of the father and the mother. But the episodes are necessarily brief. Reality intrudes. And as year succeeds year, the fantasies which make possible the relaxed companionabilities of friendship disappear. Moments of pretending, of fantasizing, and of "playing" become more and more infrequent, and finally cease. The adolescent finds friendship among true peers, and the parents find yet another "love" snatched from them.

The third love is eros—a love surrounded with romantic expectation, the state we call "being in love," the love which normally includes the dimension of sexuality. This is love which seeks completion in the beloved. It is a love which expects happiness in association with another. It is activated by longings, by desires, and by the hope of being made whole by union with another. Much more than sex is involved, although the sexual act symbolizes the joining of opposites out of which there is hope of a new whole. There are elements of this love among all parents and children, as both ancient Greeks and modern Freudians attest. Although its typical manifestations are between the lover and the beloved, the husband and the wife, there are traces of it in all relationships that involve intimacy, which includes families. Despite the sniggering of sophomore psychologists there is nothing neurotic or abnormal about it. There are moments of high ecstasy between parent and child when parenthood confers a feeling of unique wholeness. There are instances of rich sensuality between parent and child which hardly center the longings of eros, but unmistakably have something to do with them.

But adolescence brings this to a close, too. Adolescents do not want to be hugged or held by the parent. They do not want to be the "completion" of their parent's unfulfilled identity. They are feeling the tugs and pulls of eros in their bodies—and the parent is not the one to whom they look for fullfillment. In fact, all cultures have carefully hedged these feelings with formal taboos, so that there will be no experimental attempts to achieve erotic wholeness between parent and child or between brother and sister. And so this love, which is usual between husband and wife and finds expansion in parent and child, now expands no more along that line of development.

Clearly, none of the loves that nurture the life between parent and child are going to continue. There is no future possible in a continuation of any of these relationships. If affection were extended, the child would be kept dependent, and the parent enslaved. If friendship were prolonged, a life of fantasy would take over reality. If eros were encouraged, the consequences would be incest.

But there is another love. Emerson said, "When half-gods go / The gods arrive." There is a sense in which that is true here. Even though the three loves already described never actually depart— they continue to function wonderfully in fortunate lives—they do not mature without a fourth love, the love that New Testament writers designate *agape*. Without it love between a parent and adolescent becomes either desiccated and dry, there being no healthy growth to feed maturity, or bitter and resentful, as expectations are continually disappointed.

This fourth love sees the nature of the other person and acts freely to do those things which suit that nature. It is not first of all a feeling, or an experience, or a need, but a decision. It *wills* the fulfillment of the other. It is the love which is demonstrated by God for his people. It is a love which neither exploits needs nor demands gifts. It seeks to enjoy what is there in the other person and to share what one has. It is the love which Jesus exhibited in every word and act: his love freed others to be themselves in a way they could never have been without him, and allowed them to respond with a love for God which no sense of dependence or realization of duty could have created.

The Christian parent lives in a tradition which specializes in this fourth love. As the realities of adolescence make the old loves unworkable, another love is immediately at hand. Any struggle to maintain the other loves is doomed to failure. Many, of course, seem determined to continue the struggle. But they do not succeed. The sooner the old loves are given up, the better. The sooner the new love is learned the better. Leon Bloy once wrote, "A bourgeois who has not lost his illusions is like a winged hippopotamus."[2] Likewise a parent. And high on the list of illusions is the idea that the old loves can simply continue forever. The loves acquired and nurtured through the years of infancy and childhood will not work any longer for the parent; another love must be embraced and practiced —the love explicated in the Gospels, given exposition by the theologians, and preached from most Christian pulpits.

St. Paul's description of this love in 1 Corinthians 13 is often read at weddings. And most appropriately, for there is no one whose love cannot be edified, expanded, and renewed by its truth. It might, though, be even more to the point to read it to parents on the thirteenth birthday of their children as a kind of placarding of the love which assimilates the inadequacies and limitations of our natural loves, and sets our love under the power of God's love for us. It would be a signal that all examples and experiences of love we have known as children of God are at hand for use in relation to our own children.

In the transition from adolescence to adulthood youth have moments when they feel unwanted, unappreciated, unloved. Parents have corresponding experiences. For both of them affection, friendship, and eros have taken them as far as they can—it is time for *agape* to be learned. Not an easy thing, and yet not nearly as difficult as if there were no *agape* there to be experienced and learned.

7 "You're Nothing But a Hypocrite!"

As adolescents develop powers of abstraction, they learn to formulate general principles, and from them to make application in specific situations. When the principles are in algebra, they practice on problems. When the principles are moral, they practice on their parents. The parents have the not altogether welcome experience of having their own teaching redirected back to them.

❊ ❊ ❊ ❊ ❊ ❊ ❊

1. Do you ever feel that you are on trial with your children? that they are judging you, evaluating you, comparing you with other parents?
2. What accusations that your children have made of you have helped you—have been close enough to the truth to get you to see something that you wouldn't likely have seen without the pointing of their finger?
3. What accusations that your children make of you do you think are mistaken, an application of spurious standards, or the result of naiveté about the complexities of your life? When they do that, how do you respond?
4. In what areas are you in danger of being a hypocrite? areas where you are tempted to merely pretend instead of engaging in the strenuous moral effort of being a disciple?
5. Read Matthew 23. Jesus levels seven woes against the hypocrites he was living with. Which of the seven gets closest to where you are living?

❊ ❊ ❊ ❊ ❊ ❊ ❊

The lashing accusation from a teenage son or daughter, "You're nothing but a hypocrite!" is one of the most painful things a parent has to endure. It is painful because there is nearly always some truth in it. It is also the most difficult of accusations to defend oneself against. Defensive responses are usually considered additional evidence to document the accusation.

Adolescents are, as a class, moralists and idealists. They become aware of the great moral abstractions—peace, love, justice, honesty, righteousness. As children they know these things in terms of specific applications—and it was the parent who usually made the applications. Parents are, whether they self-consciously set themselves up as such or not, teachers of righteousness. They set the standards, define the limits, propose the ideals. It is natural that children come to associate the parent with the ideals. That which is said becomes identified with the one saying it.

During the years of childhood parents are accepted uncritically. Children, it is true, rebel at rules and defy commands. They disobey and ignore parents. But as they do it they do not usually mean anything *personal* about it. They are not evaluating the parental word or questioning the parental authority. And then, with the onset of adolescence, they do. It must be quite a shock to wake up one day to the realization that your parents are neither omnipotent nor omniscient (they learned, several years ago, that they were not omnipresent!). Youth begin to see a wider world of morality. They gain the ability to conceive moral *principles*. Morality, which for the child is an unorganized collection of dos and donts, begins to fit into a pattern. For instance, honesty, which for children meant not cheating on a test in school, for teenagers is understood as a principle which they can apply in any situation. It is not long until parents become one of those situations. The parents find their son or daughter scrutinizing their behavior with the moral glasses the parents themselves provided. Youth make moral judgments, using principles their parents have trained them in, on government, schools, peers: they make no exception for parents.

The stock parental response to such treatment ranges from an angry defense, to an elaborate rationalization that would do an eighteenth-century Jesuit proud, to brusque indifference. There is another response which can be developed, the response of gratitude. Gratitude that the parent now has in the home a kind of testing device which sounds the alarm when hypocrisy is detected. Parents need that. The sin of hypocrisy is one of the most difficult to detect in yourself. The one engaged in hypocrisy very quickly becomes blind to what he or she is doing. Without an outside accusation, without a jolting interruption, we can go for weeks and years thinking our religion and morals are in order. The motives of adolescents in acting as moral detectives may not be as pure as we would wish, but their function is, nevertheless, of wonderful use.

The Christian has more to fear from hypocrisy than anything else. Nothing stirred Jesus to hotter indignation. Jesus unfailingly approached the everyday sort of sinners who robbed, broke the sabbath, engaged in prostitution, and even murdered, with inviting compassion. Hypocrites got nothing but his denunciation. The fiery passage in Matthew 23 seethes with anger as Jesus lets loose a string of "woes" against those who profess one thing and do another, who talk good religion but practice none of it, who spend enormous amounts of time tidying up the externals and ignore all the internal realities that count with God.

It is salutary for every parent (especially a parent of an adolescent) to read Matthew 23 every six months or so and in the reading to substitute "parent" for "scribes and Pharisees." So instead of, "Woe to you, scribes and Pharisees, hypocrites!" it will read, "Woe to you parents, hypocrites!" The substitution is not at all farfetched. Scribes and Pharisees were by no means bad people. They were among the most responsible, moral, and respectable people in the first-century society. They provided the stable leadership that everyone needed and depended upon. Without them there would have been very little that went on that was worthwhile. Much of the same thing can be said of parents today. So why be so hard on them? Because " 'to whom much is given, of him will much be required.' " The Pharisees had been given responsibility for leading the people in the things of God. It was their task to make decisions and give guidance on morals and ritual. Anything that had to do with people as moral beings and spiritual creations was their specialty. And they gave excellent guidance. Jesus never did quarrel with their teachings. But they confused *saying* things with *being* someone. They themselves were under threat of damnation for not doing what they were saying. They had become professionalized. "Lilies that fester smell far worse then weeds."

It is interesting to observe the difference between the way the Greeks and Jesus viewed the hypocrite. In the Greek world the word was never used in a derogatory way. The word is derived from *hypokrinomai* which means "to answer back, to declaim, to give a speech." It gradually came to have a specialized use in the theater for the speeches actors gave on the stage—for the actor "spoke back" lines that had been given him by another. As the language developed, the people on the stage were given the designation *hypocrites* —the ones who skillfully declaimed in the theater the lines the dramatist had given them.[1] The theater was held in high regard among the Greeks. It was a place of high poetry and fine art. Much truth was spoken from the Greek stage. Some of the most forcible representations of human need and glory came out of the works written by Aeschylus, Sophocles, and Euripides. Naturally, those who spoke them were honored. In these performances the common people had access to the perceptions and poetry of their best artists. No one expected the actor, *the hypocrite,* to live out in his own life the truths of *Oedipus Rex* or *Seven Against Thebes.* It was enough that he speak them convincingly.

So why did Jesus not honor those in his own tradition who did the same thing? who spoke the words of Moses and Isaiah among the people? who acted out the rituals of Leviticus? who impressively gave public witness to the prayers of the fathers? who dressed in impressive, symbolical garments so that the people might not forget their origins or their destiny? If the scribes and Pharisees had lived in Athens they would have been honored all over the city for being such fine *hypocrites.* In Jerusalem they experienced the wrath of Jesus. Why the difference?

Because in Jesus the word of God became a matter of personal response between sinful people and a loving Savior. What mattered was that people respond: the inner life of faith, hope, confession, and repentance was called into being. The heart—that great Biblical metaphor for all that makes us function in relation to God—is the site for the action.

Religion is not a ritual in which some act out the truths for others, but a faith in which each person experiences what God has for her or him. All the great dramas of redemption are acted out, not on a Greek stage, but in a human heart. Anyone who brings the Greek methods into the world of faith betrays it; makes it something to be talked about instead of engaged in; makes it a matter of forms and appearances rather than of energies and commitments.

For years parents are in a position of saying things to their chil-

dren whether they, the parents, believe in them or not, whether
they feel them or not. Their own feelings, in fact, are irrelevant.
They warn their children not to cross the street, although they walk
across the street themselves. They forbid their children to use mat-
ches, although they themselves use them. They make the children
go to bed at 8 o'clock in order to get enough rest for the next day,
while they themselves stay up until midnight and are grumpy with
fatigue the next day. What is asked of the child is not imposed on
the parent—nor can it be. But the result is that parents get used to
dividing what they tell the child from what they do themselves.
They have certain principles in mind—of safety, of health, of pro-
priety—yet they apply them differently as between themselves and
the child. But that practice, as necessary and inevitable as it is in
many things, brings the parents perilously close to the state of
"scribes, Pharisees, hypocrites."

One summer, while hiking with my family in a national park in
the Rocky Mountains, I was crossing an alpine meadow with my
fourteen-year-old daughter and stopped to admire a cluster of wild-
flowers that were new to me. The meadow was profuse with them
and, not trusting my memory for a later identification, I stooped
and plucked one, and put it in my pocket. This despite the clearly
stated rules that no wild-flowers were to be picked, and that I had
for years been drumming the Sierra Club motto into my children's
heads—"Take nothing but pictures, leave nothing but footprints."
As we continued along the trail my daughter suddenly said, "Dad
you're as bad as Mr. Nixon!" (It was the summer of Watergate.) I
responded with a defense: "You have to understand the intent of the
rules; it is so other people can enjoy the flowers. But we are in a
remote part of the mountains and these flowers are plentiful, and
I very carefully took one that was in an obscure place. One of the
reasons we have parks is so people like us can come closer to this
great creation, and learn and study the handiwork of God. My
picking that little flower is really within the spirit of the entire
place." She did not respond and we walked along in silence. I don't
know if she was silent because she didn't want her father to be "as
bad as Mr. Nixon" and so accepted even bad logic as a defense
against disillusionment, or whether she was silent out of sheer em-
barrassment at her father's hypocrisy. At any rate, the farther we

walked the more smarting the accusation became. Gradually the staggering beauty of mountains and meadows wasn't available to me any more— all I was aware of was the perceptive accusation, "you're as bad as Mr. Nixon," and the lame apology I had given. Finally, I could take it no longer and said to her, "Look, I think you're right—I mean about me and Mr. Nixon. I both broke the law and violated my own principles. And I appreciate you pointing it out. People who are telling others how to behave all the time sometimes think they don't have to keep their own rules. I needed that."

In reflecting back over the incident I realized what a key role adolescence played in it. My two sons, who were pre-adolescent, would never have made the accusation—they thought everything I did was right just because I did it. My wife would never have made the accusation—she would more likely have collaborated with me, having similar interests and similar blind spots. But the peculiar vision of the adolescent perceived a relation between personal performance and the principles of morality, and was bold enough to announce the perception.

An open parent is going to be checked at many points by the adolescent. Hypocrisy is going to be noticed and challenged. I can't help but believe that it is one of the most useful and timely things our youth do for us.

I don't think, though, that simply because adolescents sometimes speak in moral tones they suddenly acquire moral authority. Their insights do not suddenly catapult them into a position of superiority. Finding stupidity, intransigence, and evil where they did not expect it—in their parents—is only the beginning of their moral education. Someday they will find it in themselves; and when they do they will no longer be kids. As Murray Kempton says, the test of maturity is the forgiveness of one's elders.[2] Youth use the pejorative "hypocrite" quite indiscriminately and often inaccurately. Sometimes they simply use it as a synonym for "sinner"—someone who is not perfect, a Christian who forgets and gets irritated and makes misjudgments. In such cases some elementary instruction in the nature of hypocrisy is in order. For the hypocrite is not a person who claims to be a Christian and who at the same time sins. All of us do that. The finest of the saints did that. Hypocrites are those who spend their time ritualizing the religious life, but with no

intention of living it, ever. They are the people who are not concerned with working out the life of faith in intimate relationships
and personal actions. Hypocrites do not sin more than others, they
pretend more. They don't fail more often; they do, though, fake it
more often. Just because our sons and daughters discover we are not
perfect does not provide them *prima facie* evidence for hypocrisy.
And they need to know that, for there is a little bit of blackmail in
every adolescent, and parents are vulnerable people.

8 "I Don't Know What I Want to Do!"

Goal confusion—not knowing what you want out of life—is a common adolescent malady. It gets in the way of everything. The future is confused, uncertain, and ominous. There are choices coming up that need to be made, there are decisions that will have to be lived with for a long time to come, and the self is not prepared. Christian hope provides the best environment in which to work through these issues.

* * * * * * * *

1. How do you feel about the future? Do you indulge in fantasies about it? What are they? Are you anxious about the future? Describe your anxieties.

2. What do your teenagers feel about the future? Are they obsessed with it? Do they avoid it? Do they think realistically about it? Are they panicked by it?

3. A large component of an adolescent's future is vocation—a vocation which is still uncertain, still undefined. What are your feelings about it? What would you like your children to do? What education do you hope they will get?

4. How do you feel about your own work? Do you enjoy what you do? What vocational disappointments do you live with? Out of your experience, what kind of guidance will you be able to give your child?

5. The Christian contribution to a mature facing of the future is summed up in the word "hope." What does the word mean to you? What do you know about it? How do your experiences of hope equip you to deal with the future?

* * * * * * * *

The "future" is a new experience for adolescents. Infants and young children live in the present. They have almost no historical sense. They are absorbed in what *is*. That is, in fact, one of the attractions of childhood—the capacity to lose oneself completely in the *now*. But in adolescence the capacity to imagine forward, to plan ahead, to anticipate, awakens. When a six-year-old boy is asked what he wants to be when he grows up and he says, "a fireman," his parents are amused. They encourage the role playing as a game, perhaps by taking him to the fire station and setting him on an engine, or buying him a fireman's hat. When a sixteen-year-old says, "fireman" the response takes the form of serious questioning: "What kind of training will you have to have? Have you looked into the pension plan? What are your chances for career development?" The "future" is no longer dreams and wishes to be indulged, but a spectrum of possibilities that must be planned for.

The future intrudes upon the adolescent from many different directions at once: there are impending choices about jobs, careers, schooling, and marriage. At the same time that there is this sudden inrush of "future," there is a corresponding feeling of helplessness, of not knowing enough, of not being adequate to make choices, of being overwhelmed by uncertainties. The situation is exacerbated by a rapidly changing world in which things don't remain stable long enough to allow for good planning. Youth know there are experts who are quite serious in predicting catastrophe within the next generation: if doomsday is around the corner what is the sense in making responsible plans for what might never take place?

The Christian church has a doctrine for equipping people to deal with the future—the doctrine of hope. Without hope a person has basically two ways to respond to the future, with wishing or with anxiety. Wishing looks to the future as a fulfillment, usually miraculous, of desire. It expends its energy in daydreaming and fantasy. Anxiety looks to the future as a demonstration of inadequacy—present weakness is projected to the point of disaster. It expends its energy in introspective fretting or distracting busyness. The prevalence, alternately, of fantasies and anxieties among adolescents is well known. The most popular form of literature among youth is science fiction, a form of fantasy which takes wishes (or fears) and projects them far into the future without the bother of figuring out intermediate steps. As for anxiety, the incidence of suicide, drug use, and emotional breakdown—all anxiety responses to a future that seems too difficult to face—is particularly high among adolescents.

Between this Scylla and Charybdis the Christian church teaches hope. Hope is a response to the future which has its foundation in the promises of God. It looks at the future as time for the completion of God's promise. It refuses to extrapolate either desire or anxiety into the future, but instead believes that God's promise gives the proper content to it. But hope is not a doctrine *about* the future: it is a grace cultivated in the present, it is a stance in the present which deals with the future. As such it is misunderstood if it is valued only for the comfort it brings; as if it should say, "Everything is going to be all right in the future because God is in control of it, therefore relax and be comforted." Hope operates differently. Christian hope alerts us to the possibilities of the future, fills the future with the promises of God, opens up the future as a field of action, and as a consequence fills the present with energy. As Jürgen Moltmann says, "The goad of the promised future stabs inexorably into the flesh of every unfulfilled present."[1]

The only person besides the adolescent more in need of grounding in Christian hope is the parent of the adolescent. The middle-aged, notoriously, are afflicted with *acedia, tristesse;* and a whole culture functions to manipulate and make a profit out of their faded hopes. As parents develop understandings and experiences of hope with their teenagers, they lay foundations which both of them need and can use to build upon in the future.

Parents have a working laboratory for developing the virtue of hope as they participate with their teenager in conversation about the future. Some of these conversations are going to be about work —the job or career that is chosen. It is a question all adolescents anticipate and know they will have to face eventually. They both look forward to it and dread it: future work is a focus for both wishing and worrying. Sometimes, in tones of lament, they will say, "I don't know what I want to do!" During this period there are suggestions to be made and ideas to be introduced that can surround the future of work with hope rather than leave it prey to either fantasy or anxiety. Christians, through the centuries, have formulated a position which views work not as a curse to which we are sentenced but as a form for both experiencing and expressing hope. Parents who are familiar with these insights will be able both to demonstrate them and converse about them. Blessed the youth who has such parents!

One thing parents can do is talk very honestly about their own experiences in work, their goals, their achievements, their disappointments and failures. If parents are willing to talk about their work and share the meaning or lack of meaning within it, they provide a conversational context in which an adolescent can begin grappling with a vocational decision. Parents don't have to be experts. They don't have to be enthusiasts in what they are doing. The important thing is that they be willing to talk about work in relationship to meaning, purpose, and life goals. What is communicated to the adolescent, then, is that there *are* goals and purposes and meanings in work. John Seeley talks about "the purpose-hunger of youth."[2] Parents can encourage a context in which a decision about a job is not an economic or an aptitude decision but a decision about the kind of life an individual wants to live.

Another thing parents can do is talk about the meaning of Christian work. When Jesus said, " 'Go . . . and make disciples of all nations, baptizing them in the name of the Father and of the Son and of the Holy Spirit, teaching them to observe all that I have commanded you; and lo, I am with you always, to the close of the age' " (Matthew 28:19–20), he wasn't giving a job description for the Christian but saying something about the stance that a Christian takes into the world of work. If we don't see how everyday work in some way or another is a response to the command " 'Go . . . and make disciples . . .' " we are going to become either very discontented with the meaning and worth of our work, or else very careless and blasé about our obedience to Christ. Many people never make the connection between their daily work and our Lord's command, and spend their working days "making a living" and their weekends and evenings trying to make up for the lack of meaning in their jobs by doing "Christian work." But that doesn't have to happen. Almost any job can be used to channel discipleship. In every decade Christians have been engaged in hundreds of occupations at all levels of society, each doing the job well "unto the Lord." And disciples have been made—who knows how many? The entire earth, not only geographically, but vocationally, has been the mission field for the Christian worker. If all this had been left only to "the religious," to ministers and missionaries, vast areas would have been neglected. Pastors and priests have had vital roles, but are neither more nor less important than any other occupation in which individuals live out their discipleship in a vocation. But how are youth to know this if they don't hear their parents or other significant adults talk about it? We tend, in our society, to exalt work as such. The Bible doesn't do that. We place a high valuation on a person who works at a good job. We pay that person a lot of money and respect. But Jesus was a carpenter and Paul was a tentmaker. Neither job was exceptional in its demands, its prestige, or its usefulness to humankind. Both jobs, though (and there are numerous other Biblical examples), became the working context for a life of witness. They used work as a context in which to obey the Great Commission. If youth don't find that context and make that connection they will only contribute another case history to the widespread unrest and job dissatisfaction that is so characteristic of today's work world.

Service is the actual work form in which the new life in Christ is shared with other people. It is the climate in which discipleship is propagated. Jesus said it many times, most memorably on the night before his crucifixion when he said, " 'I have given you an example, that you also should do as I have done to you. . . . a servant is not greater than his master.' " (John 13:15, 16) He had just washed the feet of the disciples—a menial task and certainly not a "church" job—but a job in which he was able to give himself to them in service.

For a young person who is accumulating impressions and formulating feelings about life work it is important that "servant models" be available for observation. Other models—exploitive work, dishonest work, grasping work, work that depends for its success on the weakening or lowering of others—are everywhere. It may take some ingenuity on the part of parents to provide association with people who generously use their vocational lives as forms of service, but it can be done. And when it is done youth will see concrete, daily ways in which people live out hope—lives which reach toward a fulfillment that embraces both the self and others.

In the process of doing this, encouraging (in Moltmann's words) "vocatory visions,"[3] there are three mistakes which parents need to avoid. One of them is imposing a vocation. Parents who are stuck with work they don't like because of inadequate education sometimes put a great deal of pressure on their children to achieve

scholastically and go on to college. This is done with little sensitivity or concern about what the young person actually wants or feels.
These parents aren't really concerned about the child (although
they would protest it loudly), they are remembering their own
frustrations and trying to fulfill thwarted ambitions through the life
of a son or daughter. One survey of youth showed that 65.7 percent
of the respondents complained, "my parents won't let me follow the
vocation of my interest."

Another mistake is to do the opposite and say, "I don't care what
my child does. I just want him to be happy. He can make his own
decisions." Having said that the parent stands off and offers no
guidance at all. That leaves a vacuum which will be filled swiftly by
someone else, for a great many people *are* interested in what that
young person is going to be. There are recruiters in high schools
and colleges. Pressures are exerted; advertisements are placed; peers
are persuasive. Adolescents live in a mix of vocational pressures as
they grope toward a decision. If the parents don't participate in the
process, they simply leave the field open to someone else.

A third mistake is to pepper the youth with questions: "When are
you going to make up your mind about a job?" "When are you going
to make application for college?" "When are you going to quit going
to school and start doing something useful?" Such questions are
anxiety-producing and defense-provoking, and lead nowhere.

An excellent scaffolding for building a good vocational decision
can be constructed by welding two statements together, the question from the world and the command from the church. The world
is asking, "What are you going to be?" The church is saying, " 'Go
. . . and make disciples . . . .' " The question and the command need
to be joined and firmly secured so all the planning that is done and
all the decisions that are made will be a response to both the question and the command. The expectation from school or society that
says, "Go and get a job," needs connection with the commission our
Lord gives, " 'Go . . . and make disciples . . . .' " When this connection is made in the minds of youth they will be able to decide on
something useful to do for the rest of their lives, finding both their
direction and their motivation in the Christian experience of hope.

"Can I Have
9 the Car Tonight?"

The automobile is important to youth because it symbolizes freedom and independence. It is a threat to parents because it symbolizes danger and irresponsibility. Youth look forward to the time of driving with eagerness; parents look at it with wariness and foreboding. In the confrontation between the two there are many issues of freedom, trust, and responsibility to be worked out, issues which are also matters of Christian growth.

The car has other symbolic functions: values are on exhibit. For over a decade parents have been teaching their children a value system, and one of the visual aids in that pedagogy has been the family car.

* * * * * * *

1. When did you get your first car? How did you acquire it —was it given to you or did you earn the money yourself?
2. What is your teenager's relation to the car? What does she want? What does she ask for? What does she get? What are the major areas of conflict between you?
3. What do you fear most in your teenager's use of the car? How do you communicate your fears to him?
4 What signs of responsibility do you see in your child? What signs of immaturity are most evident?
5. What, beyond a means of transportation, does your car mean to you? What personal values could others deduce from your decisions regarding cost and style in your choice of an automobile? Are these the values you want your children to embrace?
6. Discuss this statement by Max Lerner, one of the most thoughtful contemporary observers of our human condition: "Americans spend almost as much time in their cars as in their homes. Autos are no longer a luxury for an American elite; they have become a living-standard compulsive for the American masses. They fill a psychic need more important

even than adequate housing or education or health, and form a crucial test of whether your living standards make you an accepted member of the community."[1]

7. Describe a couple of turning points in your life when your "growing up" accelerated—events that symbolize for you your own maturity.

8. In what ways does your Christian growth and development in the faith help you to understand your adolescent's growth from childhood to adulthood?

* * * * * * *

The automobile, for youth, represents the adult world. Getting access to one is a quest for maturity. The adolescent wants to use the car with greater and greater frequency and with less and less restriction. Adulthood looms as a nearly-achieved destiny—when the youth is in a car adult status is confirmed.

When a young person asks, "Can I have the car tonight?" the parent needs to be ready to talk about a lot more than accessibility to the family automobile. The surprising depth of feeling that is aroused by the question (and the angry response when the answer is no) indicates that it is a "symbol question"—an apparently simple request that represents a major area of growing up. Parents will make a better response to the question if they have thought through what the car means to youth, and what it means to them as parents.

The combination, adolescents and automobiles, makes the parents uneasy. Old responsibilities for guarding and protecting the child they have reared tangle with new responsibilities to encourage independence and freedom. These two streams of parental responsibility get more than usually confused and snarled over the question of using the car, which represents danger to the parent and independence to the youth.

Since the situation is relatively new historically, parents don't have much in the way of ancient wisdom to support them. The great Biblical parents—Abraham and Sarah, Zechariah and Elizabeth, Joseph and Mary—never heard the question. And neither did our own grandparents. Which means that parents need to do their own listening, understanding, and guiding, with very little in the way of precedence to guide them.

In America achieving access to the car is a major event in the world of youth. In some primitive cultures sex is the key adolescent experience: an adolescent boy is ritually provided with an older woman who initiates him, via sex, into adulthood; an adolescent girl, at the onset of menstruation, is segregated for a period of seclusion during which she is "ritually prepared to assume her specific mode of being, that is, to become a creatress."[2] In other cultures work has been central: we know of tribes where, for boys, going hunting with the men and killing your first big animal is the initiatory event, and, for girls, being introduced into the mysteries of spinning and weaving signals acceptance into the adult community. In some societies politics has been central: arriving at voting age and casting your first vote as a citizen is the sign of acceptance into the adult world. There have been times when joining the church was the recognized ritual for initiation into adulthood.

But in America today getting your driver's license is central. Sex is fantasized, work is delayed, politics is remote, the church is vital for only a few. The automobile is a constant reality, and it represents, from the perspective of youth, anyway, the power and freedom that are prerogatives of adults. When the adolescent sits behind the wheel of an automobile, he or she is accepted as a legitimate part of adult society.

The event is public, socially sanctioned, legally circumscribed. Adolescent participation is nearly total. Recognition is immediate. The event gathers powerful symbolic energies around it. Driver education courses have replaced Samoan puberty rites and church membership services as the ritual introduction to the power, status, and freedom of adulthood. The driver's license is the passbook to maturity. It is enormously important, probably the most important cultural-social event in adolescent life. For the adolescent, accessibility to the car means accessibility to adulthood.

Until parents understand that and appreciate the implications of it they will not do well at handling the question, "Can I have the car tonight?" So it is important that they make a special effort toward sympathetic understanding. Driving a car for the parent has long been a routine operation—just like being an adult has been. But youth are on the edge of it, and very excited about it.

The parents' difficulty is that while the state is willing to certify their adolescents as licensed drivers of automobiles, and the school gives them good marks in "driver education" (treating them, in other words, as responsible adults), the parents have a lot of day-to-day evidence that their children are a long way from maturity: adolescents' emotions get out of control easily; their sense of responsibility is erratic; they unaccountably swing from apathy to exhilaration. The state and school might think it is safe to let them on the highways; the parents have doubts. Parents suspect that the State Police might have doubts too if they were regularly subjected to the sounds of slammed doors and the sight of unkempt rooms that make up the everyday landscape of the home.

For adolescents the car focuses their proximity to adulthood; for parents, their distance from it. The vision of teenagers in a car fills parents with assorted misgivings. The newsreel of the mind projects on the screen of their imagination high speeds resulting in accidents, privacy encouraging sexual encounters, easy access to corrupting associates and entertainment. The parents know that however skilled youth are in handling the mechanism of the automobile they are not yet in firm control of their own emotions, their impulses, their fantasies. And the parent knows that the car can serve as a kind of high-fidelity amplification system for a person's feelings, intentions, and moods. Inner responses are catapulted into a community fireworks display through the medium of the car. Mild anger plus a car can become manslaughter. Sexual desire plus a car can become premature sexual intimacy.

If parents are going to avoid giving an irresponsible yes to a request for the car or a rigidly restrictive no, they are going to have to find some way to discuss these things in the home. They will need to explore and accept the importance of what the car means to youth. They will want to admire and compliment the achievement which driving ability represents. But they will have to be honest and open about their own feelings and fears, and what they know about adolescent emotions and impulses.

Christians have a continuing kind of experience that helps them to understand what it means to move from childhood to adulthood. The biological-psychological move from childhood to adulthood that we call adolescence is gone through only once. By the time parents have children who are going through it, their own experience is hazy—the sharp details of their own youth years are eroded by fifteen or twenty years of other history. They have a hard time recreating in their own imagination what it was like then. But their Christian development is not fixed in the past. As Christians they are continuously involved in a similar growth movement. They are children in Christ, and they are called to move toward a maturity of discipleship: to grow up into Christ. If parents are at all serious in their Christian life they are going to experience growth pains from time to time. "Growth pains" involve finding out what it means to move from the experience of childlike trust to responsibility; from taking the experience of being loved by God and then responsibly and freely trying to love others; from trusting God personally to trusting God in the wider world of work, family, social environment. Maturity is the achievement that comes from extending the experiences of love, and intimacy, and truth beyond the privacy of the self. Christians never sever the basic relation of simple trust and dependency upon their Lord, but neither are they permitted *only* to trust and rest "in the arms of Jesus." There is the pressing call to "go into all the world and preach the gospel," to "bear one another's burdens and so fulfill the law of Christ." Because they are going through this all the time (or *can* be as growing Christians) parents have fresh, contemporary experiences to help them understand what youth is going through—the movement from the dependency experiences of childhood to the responsibility challenges of adulthood.

Youth experience in their emotions what Christians experience in their faith. The adolescent transition from the security and intimacy of the home to the challenges of work and love among people outside the home is the "life situation" stage that parallels Christian growth from trust to discipleship. The Christian parent who has a teenage son or daughter is going to read Ephesians 4:13-15 with a sharp attentiveness: "So shall we all at last attain to the unity inherent in our faith and our knowledge of the Son of God—to mature manhood, measured by nothing less than the full stature of Christ. We are no longer to be children, tossed by the waves and whirled about by every fresh gust of teaching, dupes of crafty rogues and their deceitful schemes. No, let us speak the truth in love; so shall we fully grow up in Christ." (NEB)

The automobile question can open up rich conversational relationships between youth and their parents when both are willing to follow the implications of what the car means to them. These interchanges between parent and youth can sensitize both to the feelings and aspirations that are expressed through the car. When I speed, for instance, what is being revealed in me? How does my life become altered, changed, improved, degraded by my access to the car? What does accessibility to the rapid mobility offered by the automobile do to expand my capacities for Christian self-consciousness? In what ways do my emotions, my will, my goals get expressed by this machine? How much does the car represent in terms of a tool (a vehicle for transportation), and how much in terms of a symbol (model, color, make, etc.)?

It is quite clear that the automobile serves, at least partially, to demonstrate our personal value systems, not only to the community, but to our own children. A few self-questions will open up the subject. For instance, do I lecture my children on the importance of generosity and spiritual values, and warn them against selfishness and materialism, and yet each year spend more money for the purchase of a car than in tithes and offerings in the church?

The parent can teach youth to discover in the car a useful testing place for the personality. The car can serve as litmus paper to spiritual conditions. If parents can get used to seeing the car as an amplification of feelings and decisions that provide data for evaluating themselves as responsible Christians, and if they are honest enough to permit that data to be used in conversation, they can expect to get their child to do it too.

Here is a question I have found useful to put to myself: "What do my feelings, moods, ambitions *mean* as they are given power and speed via this machine?" The car is very effective in revealing myself to me. Sometimes, for instance, I don't realize the degree of unconcern that has developed within my professed "concern for people" until I catch myself blowing my horn angrily in heavy traffic. I would never yell at a stranger in public (that would be rude, and I'm a Christian and want to share Christ's love), but because everybody else does it, I blow my horn at any stranger who offends me in a car. With excellent perception one author wrote: "Given the conditions of city traffic and bumper-to-bumper auto roads on week ends, the swollen fenders—vulnerable to the slightest dent and abrasion—make no sense in design: they make sense only in obsolescence and show. Similarly, the size and unnecessary extra engine power of the American car are intended to nourish the feeling of magnitude rather than to serve ordinary users."[3] The car, thus, amplifies and broadcasts whatever I am. Whether I am aware of it or not, my inner life is on display by means of my car. And not infrequently when I hear my feelings expressed through the traffic noise, I am faced with a need for repentance.

No one can provide a formula for when parents should say yes and when they should say no to the question, "Can I have the car tonight?" But there is a style of understanding that takes the confrontation and develops it into maturity—maturity for parents as well as youth, since the car question can set off immature responses in parent as well as youth, responses of rigid prohibition or careless, easygoing acquiescence. When it does that it only reinforces immaturity in youth. In such contexts yes and no are equally poor answers. Obviously, the question cannot just be ignored. But more than that, the prominent position the car achieves via adolescent interest makes for a wonderful opportunity—to assess the entire value system the car represents.

As a parent uneasily presides over the turbulent energies and contradictions of adolescence, the question of the car can clarify some things, particularly those that relate to maturity, in both youth and parents. As the State Police deal with driver skills, the home can deal with emotional maturity and personal responsibility and value systems. When parents and youth take the car question seriously in this context they will find it is a tool which provides them with common ground for sharing the adventure of coming to "mature manhood, measured by nothing less than the full stature of Christ." (Ephesians 4:13)

"You'll Never
10 Forgive Me!"

Given the general instability of the adolescent personality, the pressures of peers, and the moral chaos of society, there is always a chance that even the most responsible of parents may find themselves with a young person "in trouble." Parents who face such possibilities before they happen are able to pre-plan a strategy of response.

* * * * * * *

1. Were you involved in any crises as an adolescent? In what ways do you think you disappointed your parents? How did they respond?

2. As the world has increased in complexity it has diminished in wisdom. Society has become more intricate and at the same time the guidelines have become obscure. Previous generations had the advantage of a consensus on what was accepted and what was wise. The present generation gets conflicting counsel and is provided widely disparate models. Youth are called upon to make fairly sophisticated decisions in relation to machines (mostly cars), sex, entertainment, schooling—perhaps the surprising thing is that they do as well as they do. Which of these areas do you think presents the most threat to your teenager?

3. What do you fear most from the bad or unwise decisions your children may make? What consequences do you foresee? How would your personal history be affected?

4. Two common ways of responding to an unpleasant crisis are to condone or to condemn. Which would you most likely take? In what ways do you see forgiveness as different from either?

5. Read Matthew 18:21-22. How would that work out in your family?

6. Read Romans 8:28–39. In what circumstances would you find this to be an essential support?

7. What is the most striking experience of being forgiven that

you have had? What is the most significant experience of forgiving another that you have had?

* * * * * * *

Does good parenting guarantee good children? A lot of parents assume that it does: that if we do a responsible and intelligent job as mothers and fathers, if we provide a Christian home and are faithful in our prayers, if we raise our children "in the nurture and admonition of the Lord," our children are going to turn out well.

But there are precious few facts to support the assumption. One does not have to look around very long to observe some simply magnificent people who come from absolutely wretched homes. And some very troubled people who have been reared in stable, responsible, Christian homes. Even allowing for the fact that appearances are misleading—that the alcoholic father and the prostitute mother really "had a heart of gold" which accounts for the fact that their son is a kindly, successful physician; and the "pillar of the church" parents were first-class Pharisees and had a most deserved comeuppance in the sordid miseries of their daughter—still, there are enough exceptions to "good parents produce good children" that it can hardly be held as a comfortable truth.

That doesn't relieve parents from doing as good a job as possible in rearing their children. Christian parents are under solemn command to treat the children God has given them lovingly, responsibly, and seriously. But rewards are not guaranteed. And it doesn't mean that what parents do doesn't have an enormous effect on children, for it does. Good parents are an incalculable asset. Still, there are no guarantees. The finest parents in the world are no sure protection against youth's making unwise decisions or evil choices.

Christians are not determinists. We do not believe that environment makes a person a Christian, and we do not believe that heredity makes a person righteous; we do not believe that training can make a person moral, and we do not believe that baptism can create a person of faith. Christian theology maintains that every person makes his or her own decisions for or against God. Every life is an accumulation of such decisions. No one can choose right for another. The choice is free. The decision is open. Anyone, regardless of background and upbringing, can choose either way. "Multitudes,

multitudes, in the valley of decision!" (Joel 3:14) As a matter of fact, we know that people do make both kinds of choices, and that there is no neat correlation between upbringing and right choices—as if all who were reared in Christian homes make Christian choices, and all who are not reared in Christian homes do not make Christian choices.

It is important for parents to review this item of Christian doctrine at the time their children are entering adolescence. At no other time, with the possible exception of the time when the children were infants, do parents feel so responsible and at the same time so helpless, so out of control. They are apt to interpret every deviation from their teaching as evidence of parental failure: "If only we had done something differently ten years ago, perhaps our child wouldn't be doing this now."

Adolescents, almost by definition, are people experimenting with choices—flexing their will power and finding out what it means to say yes to this and no to that, feeling what it is like to do their own choosing. Parents can't have it both ways: they can't have the adolescent actually exercise the power of choice which will lead to maturity, and at the same time insist that the choices all be in line with what they, as parents, have already approved.

For the most part adolescent experiments with fledgling will power will involve matters of taste and appearance. These sometimes cause furious rows in the home, but they do not have very serious consequences. With a modest amount of good will and good humor, things proceed fairly well. But sometimes decisions are made by youth which will involve them in serious difficulty. A bad decision about sex may result in an unexpected and unwanted pregnancy. A careless decision about driving may lead to an accident in which someone is seriously injured or killed. A muddled decision about drugs may end up in arrests, jail, and the courts. Adolescence is an age of extremes: there are soaring flights to the best, but there are also plummeting descents to the worst. Usually these alternating ups and downs are restricted to the world of the imagination and the emotions; but occasionally they get acted out. And when they do there can be trouble.

When an adolescent decision has produced consequences which seem disastrous and irreversible there is usually a conclusion of despair: "you can never forgive me!" Youth are aware that they are not only the product of parental prayer but the focus of parental hopes. The prayers and promises have been channeled into their bodies and spirits. And if, now, by their bad decision their parents' expectations are shattered—" . . . after such knowledge, what forgiveness?"[1]

Even though many parents, perhaps the majority, do not have to face the question, it is always a possibility. So pre-planning is wise: every parent should realistically face the possibility that the "worst" could in fact happen in this family, and have thought about what kind of response would be best.

A Kierkegaardian insight helps here, namely, that catastrophe can be a means of grace.[2] It can be an instrument used by God by which we can cease floating passively on all manner of external attractions. It is by the grace of catastrophe that people sometimes come to themselves and see what is before them as if for the first time. Catastrophe can, like a mighty wind, blow away the abstracting veils of theory and ideology and enable our own sovereign seeing.

The ways in which parents can respond to the crises in which parental standards have been grossly violated, or an element of personal catastrophe has been introduced, fall into one of three categories: condone, condemn, and forgive. The first two are common but highly destructive to family relationships; the third is uncommon but wonderfully redemptive.

One parental response is simply to condone. The parent thinks, "If I had done a better job as a parent, he would not be in the trouble he is in now. So it is really my fault. I have no right now to reject him for what he has done; his failures are only an extension of my own. 'The sins of the fathers are being visited on the sons . . . .' " The parents try to smooth over the crisis. They try to ameliorate the consequences. They try to take the sting out of whatever suffering or punishment is involved. Insofar as possible they act as if it never happened.

This is understandable, but it is wrong. One reason it is wrong is that one of the assigned tasks of youth is to learn to take responsibility for their sin—not to blame, or project, or excuse, but to discover that they are strong enough, have enough worth, to survive sin and choose righteousness. Another reason that it is wrong is that its premise is shaky. There are no perfect parents. The best of parents make many damaging mistakes through the first twelve or thirteen years of a child's life. All parents are implicated in their children's sins. Christian teaching has always insisted that none of us loves alone and none of us sins alone. The body of Christ is intricately interdependent, even in its sins. Christians go so far as to identify their own responsibility with what happened at first-century Calvary: "Who was the guilty? Who brought this upon Thee? Alas, my treason, Jesus, hath undone Thee! 'Twas I, Lord Jesus, I it was denied Thee: I crucified Thee."[3] But by admitting to a responsibility in whatever wrong has come to light, we do not improve things by condoning it. By saying, "It doesn't really matter," what we are, in effect, saying is, "When you really look at it it wasn't all that bad, therefore my child is not as guilty as you might think—and neither am I."

Another response is to condemn. Condemnation rejects the offenders and refuses to have anything to do with them. The most dramatic form of this is the funeral service conducted by some Jewish families for a son or daughter who has married a Gentile. From that moment on the child is "dead"—there is to be no more relationship, no conversation, no exchange of love or hate, praise or recrimination. Condemnation is complete and the separation is total. Christians do not have formal religious rites to solemnize such an act of condemnation but they have emotional rites which accomplish the same purpose. In one way or another the child is cut off and disowned. The unspoken premise behind condemnation is that parenthood is not a relationship but a contract. Being a child in such a home is subject to certain conditions: when the conditions are not kept the parent is no longer under obligation to be a parent.

Like condoning, condemnation also has a large accumulation of guilt behind it. But it is unacknowledged guilt. The adolescent publicizes a streak of irresponsibility or criminality in the parents, and the parents want to get rid of it so that they won't have to face it in themselves any more. By projecting it completely on the child, and then banishing the child from their presence, they have exorcised it from themselves. Condemnation is the act in which we take the occasion of someone else's sins to get rid of our own, purging what we don't like about ourselves.

Condoning is the way of the sentimental humanist, the person who cannot bear to see others suffer the consequences of their own actions, and wants to make everything all right with mercurochrome and band-aids. Condemning is the way of revengeful barbarians, people who cannot bear to face themselves, and who want to make everything all right by getting rid of the offense. Condoning and condemning are both wrong for the same reasons: they refuse to take seriously the integrity of the other person, and to accept the fact that personal choice has personal consequences; they refuse to accept children as persons in their own right and not just extensions of the parent; and they refuse to take seriously the promises of God, to believe that God is capable of bringing good out of evil, healing out of suffering, peace out of disorder, resurrection out of crucifixion. They refuse to believe in Jesus Christ.

The Biblical narration of King David's responses to the crimes of his two eldest sons demonstrates how *not* to do it. When the eldest son, Amnon, raped his sister Tamar, David did nothing. "When King David heard of all these things, he was very angry; but he did nothing to harm his son Amnon, for he loved him, because he was his firstborn." (2 Samuel 13:21, LXX) By doing nothing he condoned it. He refused to face the enormity of the crime, to let justice take its course, to share the agony of the wrong. He responded in an opposite way when his next son, Absalom, taking justice into his own hands, murdered Amnon. This time David's response was condemnation: Absalom was banished into exile for three years. Through the intervention of a friend he was allowed to come back to Jerusalem, but still David would not speak to him or see him. He rejected him completely and cut him off from all relationship. The two responses, condoning and condemning, are really not so different—the same man was quite capable of either response. David's character did not change between the two incidents: the same man who condoned later condemned. The responses are similar in that neither deals with what happened in any responsible or personal way. At bottom there is something cowardly in the way David, alternately indulgent and harsh, dealt with his sons. One can't help conjecture that if David had handled the crises of Amnon and Absalom differently the days that followed would have been more pleasant for him.

We don't know if there were things David could have done to

prevent Amnon's rape of Tamar and Absalom's murder of Amnon
—there is much we don't know and guesses are perhaps futile. We
do know, though, that there was a very different way to respond
to the crimes once they were committed. And that is the way of
forgiveness.

Forgiveness is not a midpoint between condoning and condemning. It is not a balance between something gentle and something
harsh. It is not an apothecary's mixture of two parts acceptance and
one part punishment. It is something entirely different. It is what
God has shown us as his way of dealing with the sin which violates
truth, the sin which destroys love, the sin which disappoints hope.

The only way to understand forgiveness is to understand it as
what God does for us through Jesus Christ. Forgiveness is not a
human act; it is not what we do to repair the damage our sins have
caused. It is a divine act. It is what God does to deal with the mess
of our sins. Insofar as we can engage in it at all it is as participants
in what God is doing in Jesus Christ.

The act of forgiveness begins by accepting the sin, whatever it is.
It does not blink the sin, it does not obscure it, it does not excuse
or modify or explain it: it faces it. And it accepts the consequences
of the sin. Whatever suffering, whatever penalties, whatever dis-
comfort, whatever inconvenience that proceed from the sin, they
are also accepted. What else was the cross but an act of enormous
courage, accepting the results of sin?

Forgiveness proceeds by accepting the person who committed the
sin. It aggressively initiates a new movement of love toward that
person. It gathers him, or her, back into the relationship of love,
saying, "*You* are what is real, not the sin. Nothing you or anyone
else can do will separate you from me."

The word "forgiveness" has been watered down by journalistic
cant and careless practice. It frequently means no more than, "I'll
let it go this time—I won't let it bother me—but don't do it again."
It is the verbal equivalent to a shoulder shrug. So there needs to be
repeated return to the New Testament to renovate the word, to
discover its vitality, its strength, its power, its versatility; to realize
that it is the most creative act anyone can engage in; to know that
more new life springs from acts of forgiveness than anything else;
and to believe that the parent who is called on to engage in an act

of forgiveness is in a, literally, godlike position.

Parents are in a position to forgive when they remember two things. One, the child that I am rearing is God's child. God loved the child before I did; he will continue this love long after I am gone. Two, God's method of dealing with sin, even the most destructive kind, is forgiveness. I am not going to be able to improve on God's methods.

Howard Clinebell says, "Family life offers our best opportunities for 'covenants of intimacy' in our culture; it is important, therefore, that the Good News come alive in the dailiness of family relationships."[4] Forgiveness is the act which makes bad news convertible to good news by providing the opening for the Holy Spirit to take episodes of adolescent sin and make them into stories of mature love.

Conclusion

A search of Scripture turns up one rather surprising truth: there are no exemplary families. Not a single family is portrayed in Scripture in such a way so as to evoke admiration in us. There are many family stories, there is considerable reference to family life, and there is sound counsel to guide the growth of families, but not a single model family for anyone to look up to in either awe or envy.

Adam and Eve are no sooner out of the garden than their children get in a fight. Shem, Ham, and Japheth are forced to devise a strategy to hide their father's drunken shame. Jacob and Esau are bitter rivals and sow seeds of discord that bear centuries of bitter harvest. Joseph and his brothers ring changes on the themes of sibling rivalry and parental bungling. Jesse's sons, brave and loyal in service of their country, are capricious and cruel to their youngest brother. David is unfortunate in both wives and children—he is a man after God's own heart and Israel's greatest king, but he cannot manage his own household.

Even in the family of Jesus, where we might expect something different, there is exposition of the same theme. The picture in Mark, chapter three, strikes us as typical rather than exceptional: Jesus is active healing the sick, comforting the distressed, and fulfilling his calling as Messiah, while his mother and brothers are outside trying to get him to come home, quite sure that he is crazy. Jesus' family criticizes and does not appreciate. It misunderstands and does not comprehend.

The Biblical material consistently portrays the family not as a Norman Rockwell group, beaming in gratitude around a Thanksgiving turkey, but as a series of broken relationships in need of redemption, after the manner of William Faulkner's plots in Yoknapatawpha County.

At the very least, this means that no one needs to carry a burden of guilt because his or her family is deficient in the sweetness and light that Christian families are supposed to exhibit. Since models for harmonious families are missing in Scripture (and for that omission I am repeatedly grateful to the Holy Spirit), we are free to pay attention to what *is* there—a promise of new community which experiences life as the household of faith, a family in Christ. Life together consists of relationships which are created not by blood (at least not by our blood) but by grace. We get along not because we are good but because we are forgiven.

In this new community, created by the Holy Spirit and called the church, much of the vocabulary used to describe relationships comes from the family as we already know it: brothers, sisters, fathers, and mothers. The message seems to be something along these lines. What you never managed in your own families naturally, you may now have in the new community supernaturally. All that was lost at Eden is regained at Gethsemane. Relationships learned at the cross of Christ, the ways of love and the techniques of forgiveness, will give you the brother and sister you longed for, the son and daughter you desired. What you learn in the community of faith you will then be able to take back into your natural families of sons and daughters, of fathers and mothers.

We are faced, daily, with the reality that something has gone wrong with our families. Our children fight and quarrel; our parenting misfires. We are involved in failure, and we feel guilty. Something *has*, of course, gone wrong with the family, but it went wrong long before we came on the scene. It is futile to complain or feel guilty; we can, though, go to work and nurture family life on the new grounds provided by the Holy Spirit. Blood relationships are transformed into relationships of grace. Our natural families are informed and redeemed by the same principles that are foundational in the community of the Holy Spirit, the church.

But it is not easy to acquire these Biblical perspectives. It is especially difficult when we are isolated from others and confined within the structures of our natural family. That is why it has seemed to me so important to encourage "parent coalitions," gatherings of Christians engaged to discover and appropriate the promises and gifts of God as they are learned through the forms of family life.

Charles Williams, I think more than any other Christian in our time, has shown the centrality of what he calls "substituted love" (and what theologians in the Reformation traditions have named "the priesthood of all believers"). Williams' exposition of the doctrine in his novels and his poetry showed both how necessary and how attractive it is to "bear one another's burdens." (Galatians 6:2) He invited Christians who were faced with difficulties, whether slight or heavy, to enter into "compacts." "Compacts," he wrote in his essay "The Way of Exchange," "can be made for the taking over of the suffering of troubles, and worries, and distresses, as simply and as effectually as an assent is given to the carrying of a parcel. . . . To begin the way in small things conveniently is better than to dream of the remote splendours of the vicarious life; not that they are likely in any case to seem very splendid when they come. To begin by practising faith where it is easiest is better than to try and practise it where it is hardest. There is always somewhere where it can be done."[1]

Since the burden of parenthood is particularly onerous to many during the time their children move through the years of adolescence, I have hoped, by describing some of the motions of that process and by inviting parents to meet together, to initiate acts of burden-sharing, "compacts" of substituted love. Where two or three —and eight or ten—gathered together in our Lord's name we learned through honest discussion, serious Scripture reading, and faithful prayer, the inner dynamics of the family of God which is the church. Sometimes we found that we also became more skilled in love and practiced in pardon, and so were able to live with one another and with our sons and daughters in happier ways, and that was so much the better.

It is this second community with its origins at Pentecost that releases energies of redemption, not the first whose roots are in Eden. And so it is with the presuppositions of faith that I have approached the entire matter of the parent and the adolescent. It is more important, I think, that families be used as places to develop faith than that the faith be used as a resource to develop families. For it does no good to improve the family if we only make a household god out of our success. Our Lord, who wills our love for one another, also gave us solemn warning, " 'he who loves father or mother more than me is not worthy of me; and he who loves son or daughter more than me is not worthy of me.' " (Matthew 10:37)

Notes

Epigraph

1. Karl Barth, *Church Dogmatics* (Edinburgh: T. & T. Clark, 1961), III/4, p. 238.

Introduction

1. Thornton Wilder, *The Eighth Day* (New York: Harper and Row, 1967), pp. 297-298.
2. C.S. Lewis, *Letters to an American Lady* (Grand Rapids, Mich.: William B. Eerdmans, 1967), p. 44.
3. *The New Oxford Book of English Verse*, ed. Helen Gardner (New York: Oxford University Press, 1972), p. 930.
4. John Henry Newman, *An Essay on the Development of Christian Doctrine* (Garden City, N.Y.: Doubleday Image Book, 1960), p. 63.

Chapter 1: "I'll Dress the Way I Want!"

1. Erik Erikson, *Insight and Responsibility* (New York: W. W. Norton & Co., 1964), p. 90.
2. W. B. Yeats, "A Dialogue of Self and Soul," *Collected Poems* (New York: The Macmillan Co., 1959), p. 230.
3. Eugen Rosenstock-Huessy, *I Am an Impure Thinker* (Norwich, Vermont: Argo Books, 1970), pp. 41, 42.

Chapter 3: "You Can't Make Me!"

1. Lionel Whiston, *Are You Fun to Live With?* (Waco, Tex.: Word Books, 1963), p. 50.

2.   George Eliot, *Middlemarch*, Book II, Chapter 18.
3.   John Updike, *Museums and Women and Other Stories* (New York: Alfred A. Knopf, 1972), p. 80.
4.   Erik Erikson, *Young Man Luther* (New York: W. W. Norton & Co., 1958), pp. 69, 70.

Chapter 4: "You Wouldn't Understand!"

1.   John Henry Newman, *op. cit.*, p. 223.
2.   Lewis Mumford, *Technics and Human Development* (New York: Harcourt, Brace and Jovanovich, Inc., 1967), p. 13.

Chapter 5: "You Never Trust Me!"

1.   Howard Clinebell, *Basic Types of Pastoral Counseling* (Nashville: Abingdon Press, 1966), p. 97.

Chapter 6: "If You Loved Me, You'd Let Me!"

1.   C. S. Lewis, *The Four Loves* (London: Geoffrey Bles, 1960), p. 43.
2.   Leon Bloy, quoted in M. C. D'Arcy, *The Mind and Heart of Love* (New York: Meridian Books, 1956), p. 195.

Chapter 7: "You're Nothing But a Hypocrite!"

1.   Ulrich Wilckens, *Theological Dictionary of the New Testament*, ed. Gerhard Friedrich (Grand Rapids, Mich.: William B. Eerdmans, 1972), Vol. VIII, pp. 559-560.
2.   Murray Kempton, quoted by Garry Wills, *Nixon Agonistes* (New York: Houghton Mifflin Co., 1970), p. 601.

Chapter 8: "I Don't Know What I Want to Do!"

1.   Jürgen Moltmann, *Theology of Hope* (London: SCM Press, 1967), p. 21.
2.   John R. Seeley, *The Americanization of the Unconscious* (New York: International Science Press, 1967), p. 396.
3.   Moltmann, *op. cit.*, p. 198.

Chapter 9: "Can I Have the Car Tonight?"

1. Max Lerner, *America as a Civilization* (New York: Simon and Schuster, 1957), p. 96.

2. Mircea Eliade, *Rites and Symbols of Initiation* (New York: Harper and Row, 1958), p. 42.

3. Lerner, *op. cit.*, pp. 867-868.

Chapter 10: "You'll Never Forgive Me!"

1. T. S. Eliot, "Gerontion," *Collected Poems 1909–1962* (New York: Harcourt, Brace and World, 1963), p. 30.

2. Søren Kierkegaard, referred to by Lewis Jerome Taylor, Jr., "Walker Percy and the Self," *Commonweal* (May 10, 1974), p. 234.

3. Johann Heerman, trans. Robert Bridges, *The Hymnal* (Philadelphia: Presbyterian Board of Christian Education, 1933), p. 158.

4. Clinebell, *Basic Types of Pastoral Counseling*, p. 98.

Conclusion

1. Charles Williams, *Selected Writings* (London: Oxford University Press, 1961), p. 128.